Go for it!

7.7.7

PLAY NICE MAKE MONEY

THE CASE FOR AN ETHICAL BUSINESS MODEL AS THE MOST EFFECTIVE ROUTE TO PROFITABILITY

W.T. MCKIBBEN

THE GREAT LAKES GROUP
BUFFALO, NEW YORK

THE GREAT LAKEƒ GROUP

PO Box 33, Buffalo NY, 14072-0033 UƒA
Telephone 716.883.4695   FAX 716.829.7363
To contact us or to order copies of this book
ƒpecial pricing available for bulk orders.
Visit www.Ethics-Guru.com or Call Toll Free 1.877.619.2793

ISBN – 13   978-1-60402-412-8

ISBN – 10   1-60402-412-8

Library of Congress Control Number: 2007931182

As is every word I write, this book is dedicated to my editor, the love of my life, my life partner,

Carolyn Aylor McKibben

There would be no book without her support and guidance. Her magic and editing skills are apparent throughout this work.

CONTENTS

Always do right—this will gratify some
and astonish the rest.
Mark Twain

TAKE AWAYS!

If you do not read another word in this book, take these along.

o   Understand the impact of an ethical business model. It is the
closest thing to a sure-fire road to higher profits. By harvesting
the bounty of ethically driven self-preservation and self-interest,
it brings a wide range of economic and social benefits to every
one it touches.

o   Understand where an ethical culture begins if it is to flourish.
At the top.

o   Communications professionals must be in the fore to mark the
ethical line in the sand. They are the corporate responsibility
troops on the front line, they are Paul Revere, the canaries in the
coal mine. As lawyers mark the line to keep you out of court (or
jail), the communications pros mark the line —somewhere way
north of that— that protects and enhances both reputation and
profitability. Remembering the distinction between these two
valuable and important but very different disciplines is critical
to corporate health and well-being.

o   Embrace benevolent capitalism. A form of capitalism that is not
just the best way to make the most money, it is the key to overcoming many of the evils of the world. A prosperous, content
middle class does not breed terror. Successful trading relationships defuse a toxic atmosphere where war can brew.

o   We have only begun to create a world where every human being
can develop their full potential. About a half-billion of those of
us who inhabit the earth earn $15,000 a year or more. Three
times that many, a billion and a half, earn between $1,500 and
$15,000 a year.

Two-thirds of the people on the earth, four billion, earn less than
$1,500 a year. Think what giving those people a chance to achieve
their potential could do to change the world. They are as smart
as the rest of us. They are at least as good as the rest of us.
There is no force on earth better equipped or more likely to
succeed at bringing prosperity to mankind than benevolent
capitalism doing the right thing.

The truth of the matter is
you always know the right thing to do.
The hard part is doing it.
Norman Schwarzkopf
U.S. Army, Retired

INTRODUCTION

So the question is, do corporate executives, provided
they stay within the law, have responsibilities in their
business activities other than to make as much money
for their stockholders as possible? And my answer to
that is, no they do not. [1]
Milton Friedman, 20th Century Economist

True, so far as it goes. But "how" to make as much money
as possible is the trick. History and current practice show
that the business leaders who put making money last and
work for the good of all, make the most money possible for
their stockholders. In this century the ethical business model
is the runaway profit leader.
W.T. McKibben, 21st Century Ethics Guru

This is a book about following our most basic instinct, self-preservation.
Many believe that "Looking out for #1" means doing what you have to
do to "get yours." What if the best way to "get yours" was the exact
opposite? What if the best way to "get yours" was to be sure everyone
you dealt with "got theirs"? What if following the highest ethical standards
was the best and fastest way to success in business? I've always believed
that to be true. I now feel there is solid evidence that it is true. Come
with me on a journey through time and examine the evidence that doing
the right thing is the right thing for you.

Greed is so yesterday! Trying to run a business focused on the bottom
line is like trying to break par by sitting in the club house looking at
the scorecard. You have to get out on the course and play the game.

Ethics is a broad and broadly misunderstood subject. I like the *American
Heritage Dictionary* definition, "A set of principles of right conduct."[2]
Doing the right thing. While this is the foundation of my position, this

---

[1] *New York Times Magazine.* 9/13/1970

[2] Ethics. Dictionary.com. *The American Heritage® Dictionary of the English Language, Fourth Edition.*
Houghton Mifflin Company, 2004. http://dictionary.reference.com/browse/Ethics (accessed: 3/24/07).

book is an exploration of ethics not as a moral principle, but as a sound business practice. It explores a business model that strives first to do the right thing in all things. A business model that puts profit last, and in so doing achieves levels of profit exceeding the wildest dreams of those who place profit at the forefront of their business model.

A business model that attracts and retains customers. A business model that attracts the best and the brightest employees and strives to give them every opportunity to grow and control their destiny. A culture that motivates them to be productive and loyal. A business model that seeks to deliver the best services, the finest goods, at pricing that is fair to the customer and to the suppliers and vendors who support it. A business model that realizes the importance of citizenship in the community and the importance of protecting the environment. A business model anyone would be proud to lead or be a part of.

Enron, Adelphia, WorldCom, and other headline-grabbing miscreants have created a public perception that the way to succeed in business is to follow the twist on the Golden Rule that says, "Do unto others *before* they do unto you." Sayings like "Nice guys finish last" and Hollywood depictions of scheming, unscrupulous business leaders have many people believing that the business community is made up largely of those types.

Worse, we have young people coming into our workforce believing that this cutthroat behavior is the norm. Buying into the idea that the only way to get ahead is at the expense of others. The facts say otherwise. In truth, the most effective way to succeed in business is to consistently do the right thing. And it always has been. These pages represent my passion to document the fact that benevolent capitalism is ultimately more profitable and satisfying than any alternative. That a collaborative, nurturing culture spawns productivity and profit. And it is loads more fun.

As General Schwarzkopf points out, that doesn't mean it is easy. Nothing worthwhile is easy. Sometimes it is hard to do the right thing. When we make a mistake on the job, it is hard to own up to it and take the hit. It seems easier to cover up errors and hope no one will find you out. I suspect we have all done exactly that. But we soon discover that owning up to our mistakes is an important step in building the trust of our fellow workers, our employer, and our partners, the stockholders.

In truth, it makes life easier in every aspect. And, it is way better than being caught trying to cover up. If you are lucky, you learn early on in life that no matter how hard you try to cover something up, odds are you will get caught. Owning up to mistakes is even more important if you are a leader. It builds team spirit and by example encourages your people to be just as forthcoming.

Tom Friedman points out in his book on globalization, *The World Is Flat,* that "search engines flatten the world by eliminating the valleys and peaks, all the walls and rocks, that people used to hide inside of, atop, behind, or under in order to mask their reputations. In a flat world you can't run, you can't hide." [3]

Most of us realize that the sooner a misstep is acknowledged and corrected, the better it is for everyone and the business. Learning from our mistakes is one of the ways we grow the business. After several decades as a journalist, business person, and consultant, I'm not only sure that doing the right thing is good for business, I'm convinced the majority of businesses operate closer to that standard than the robber baron model commonly depicted. Think what our world would be like if everyone "got it."

The evidence is overwhelming. Study after study, book after book, article after article offer testimony to the success of the ethical business model. In part four of this book I share a few of the more outstanding examples of literature and research that make it clear that no matter how you measure it, choosing the high road is best, especially for the bottom line. It has been difficult to hand off this book to the printer as fresh pieces of research supporting its premise seem to turn up every day.

The existence of hard evidence first came to me from writer David Wolfe, who along with Raj Sisodia of Bentley College and Jag Sheth of Emory University, set out to identify and study outstanding corporate citizens. Companies that treat their employees, their suppliers, their customers, their communities, and the environment with great respect. They call these companies (and the book based on their study) *Firms of Endearment.* These companies are at this point in time –in these authors' view– the best in the land based on these factors. Then almost as an afterthought they looked at the financial performance of the public companies on their list and found that they returned eight times

---

[3] Thomas L. Friedman, *The World Is Flat* (New York: Farrar, Straus, & Giroux, 2005), 158.

as much over the preceding ten years as did the Standard & Poor's 500. That's eight times the average of the overall list, not eight times the worst companies on the S&P!

It all comes down to what my Daddy often asked, "Why wouldn't you seek out an honest business man?" I hold that this is what we are all looking for. As customers we want to be dealt with in a fair and honest manner. As workers we hope for fair treatment and both financial and emotional recompense for our efforts. As vendors and suppliers we want our efforts appreciated and a chance to make a reasonable profit.

As stockholders and lenders we expect the best return on our funds, and we want to be proud of the businesses we own. As neighbors we expect businesses to be good citizens and support our community, and we expect respect for our needs and the environment. We want those we deal with in business to Play Nice.

This book is not an apologia for businesses large or small; it is an attempt to provide support for those who find themselves unsure about these issues. And to assure those entering our economy that doing the right thing is the right thing for your future. Does this mean that it always works out that way, that if you play nice you will always be a winner?

Of course not.

There will always be those who buy into the barracuda school of business practices. Hopefully, a lot fewer once the ethical business model is more universally understood. Sometimes the barracudas will win. Conversely, some good guys will end up last. But the vast majority will not. And even when good guys fail, they will at least be able to look at themselves in the mirror and look their children in the eye.

Does anyone really need more than that? ✌

*It takes 20 years to build a reputation
and five minutes to ruin it.*

PART ONE

NOTHING NEW

Doing business with those who
deal off the top of the deck has
always been the way to build a
successful and profitable business.

What I am suggesting is not a new idea. It probably goes back to the first leader to form a collaborative hunting party to feed the women and kiddies back home in the cave. I'm sure he found that being a nice Neanderthal got him a lot more helpers and brought home more game than bad-ass Org on the other side of the mountain who put his group together with the help of a strong arm, a big club, and a know-it-all leadership model.

I am well aware that there were advanced civilizations in some parts of the world while in others folks were still grunting and throwing rocks at each other. Even the Romans were pretty primitive compared to the cultures in China, India, and just across the Mediterranean in Africa at that time.

Since the records from these periods are a little sketchy, however, I am starting my documentation of the nice guy business model with the second century of the industrial revolution in merry old England and here in America. That's when things really got rolling and big industrial organizations began to appear. It happens to coincide with the modern democratic era as it was evolving in the United States.

The first chapter offers some of the factors in my background that impacted my view of how a business should function. Chapters 2 through 5 trace the history of benevolent management through the lives of four business leaders who stand as examples from the 1700s to the 1900s. There were surely others, but these four make my point that from the beginning the high road has been rewarding personally and financially. And now there is more than this kind of anecdotal evidence to support that view. Evidence that should convince any thinking person that an ethical business model beats the pants off all the alternatives.

Hopefully, we can build on the stories of these successful business pioneers who chose to play nice and embolden those starting out in business today. It's nothing new; playing nice has always been the best business model. It can make you more money than any other plan, and it is infinitely more fun and more satisfying. ℰ

Each man cares that his neighbor shall not cheat him.
Then comes a day when he begins to care
that he does not cheat his neighbor.
And then all goes well.
He has changed his market-cart into a chariot of the sun.
Ralph Waldo Emerson

CHAPTER ONE

THE ACCIDENT OF BIRTH

We are the product of where we were
born, of those who preceded us, and
of those who shaped us in our youth.

My mother regularly expressed thanks that her forbearers had chosen
to come to America. When I hear so-called self-made business people
brag "I could have made it anywhere," I am wont to ask how well they
would have done had they been born in a desperately poor third world
village. We are all positioned in life by our place of birth and a host of
other factors beyond our control. The outcomes are determined as much
by luck as by anything. You can succeed on nothing but luck, but you
can't succeed without a little luck, if nothing else where you were born.

Those who choose to measure success by position or material gain will
be disappointed. I have known many people who gained the highest
positions in business and many people who were very rich. Neither of
these factors held the key to happiness for any of them. In fact, more
than a few found nothing but grief in power and wealth. This is not to
say that you cannot be happy if you are successful or have money. It's
just a lot harder. Money and power are satisfying only if they do not
control you. Unless you are willing to walk away from them if they
interfere with your ethics, at best you will be unhappy. At worst they
will destroy you, your dreams, and everything you love. In a word, the
only way to be happy with money and power is to know what they are
worth —nothing— and be willing to cast them aside.

I offer that for openers because I think that those who fail to do the right
thing often believe that's the route to power and money. Some of them
succeed in reaching these goals. Along the way they rationalize their
actions as "what I had to do." But in their innermost heart of hearts
they know they did what they did for the power, glory, and money. And
they cover the empty spot in their hearts with excuses and excess.

I can promise that doing the right thing will make you happier. I cannot promise that you will make money. If you work hard and are lucky you might achieve power and wealth and even fame as well, but in any case you will live a fulfilling life if you choose the high road. I'm just saying that your chances are as good or better on the high road and that you will end up making more money if you succeed. Living a happy life is not what this book is about. It's about doing the right thing because it is the best way to succeed in business. While it is sometimes difficult, it is the best way to reach those goals, even if you don't care about satisfaction and happiness. It's a bonus. Get used to it, you'll like it.

My parents were born in the "Gay Nineties," my father in 1893, my mother in 1895. They grew up on small family farms a couple miles apart in a Western Pennsylvania Scotch-Irish culture built around the Presbyterian faith and far removed from the lifestyle that gave the era its name. After they married in 1920 they stayed on the farm until they were well into their thirties. Father farmed and Mother took the train from the Ivywood station near the farm into Pittsburgh each day to her job as a secretary at the booming H. J. Heinz Company.

As they approached their forties, still childless, they moved off the farm to the county seat, the small community of Butler, Pennsylvania. To their delight they finally had a child. Mother, as was the custom in that time, left her secure position as secretary to the second in command at Heinz. A month after my birth the nation was plunged into the Great Depression and Father found himself out of work. It would be two years before he found another position. But through it all I could not have been a more cherished child, perhaps their greatest gift. It never occurred to me that I was deprived.

All these factors influenced my life in ways that I am still discovering. While Father's spirit was crushed by the depression, he never allowed it to get him down or incapacitate him. He went out every morning looking for a way to earn an honest dollar here and there. The outlook on risk that he gained from the depression was the opposite of the fear he brought out of it. For the rest of his life fear held him back from taking financial risks. However, the lesson he passed on to me was just the opposite —don't be afraid. "If you take a risk and lose, financially you are just back where you started," he finally decided. He pointed out that he knew how bad things could get, and that it wasn't that bad.

While some might correctly say that I took that advice way too literally, I have certainly enjoyed a much better life than I might have, had I played it safe. I passed the risk-taking gene to my children. My first-born, Mark, landed a dream job in the early days of satellite digital transmission and then went out on his own to build a groundbreaking company that helped to create the cable network infrastructure across America. He took bold risks; he has reaped both success and happiness.

The second, my daughter Tracy, rode the entrepreneurial roller coaster with me before taking some time to raise her boys. Bob, the youngest, left a trail of success behind in a large national organization and rolled the dice with some partners that they could grow a tiny company they took over on a wing and a prayer. He now heads that company with hundreds of employees in branches sprawled over three states. So far all three have found satisfaction and a measure of financial success as well. They have taken both financial risks and the risks inherent in doing the right thing, a path I consider less risky than the alternative.

I learned that lesson first from my parents. Father always looked for the honest merchant and in his life strived to do the right thing. My mother had the example of H.J. Heinz, who had suffered bankruptcy and came back to build a great company based on doing the right thing. Working day-in and day-out quite literally outside Heinz's office door, she knew that he and the other executives walked the walk. Year after year she observed the ethical business model Heinz pioneered. She personally benefited from the culture Heinz radiated throughout his company. She saw what it did, not just for those at the executive level where she worked, but for everyone throughout the organization right down to those in the most humble positions. They were all treated with the same courtesy and respect.

I was weaned on what I would later come to understand as an ethical business model. Growing up, I saw those who didn't follow it as crooks, and I guess I still do. I by no means am suggesting that I have lived a perfect life, or that I have never crossed the line or lacked the courage to the right thing. I am just pointing out that I keep trying. Whatever I have achieved in creating a series of workplaces based on doing the right thing is the result of a myriad of influences that shaped me over the years. However, the foundation for the ethical business model I propose began at home.

Another crucial lesson came while I was still in my twenties. I found myself in the forefront of the rock and roll revolution as a member of the top tier of a management team running one of the hottest and most successful radio groups in the nation. I had primary responsibility for the day-to-day operation of the group's anchor station and oversight of another station, along with a number of responsibilities at corporate level, including compliance with Federal Communications rules and regulations. A task I found easier when I set the standard way above the edge of the law.

Notice that I used the word "responsibility." There was no question that the "Buck Stops Here" sign was clearly on my desk. What was missing was any authority to impose, carry out, or enforce any activity. The final word lay with my boss, who periodically pointedly reversed my decisions. I had no "Command or Control" and everyone knew it. At the time it was very frustrating. I had to learn to temper my actions and be sure that I had everything in hand –including how others in the organization might feel– before I set something in motion. And then I had to convince everyone that it was the best course for us to take. They all knew that I had no teeth, so I had to use consensus and reason to lead.

It may have been the best thing ever for my career. It taught me that a leader with a willing, enthusiastic team beats command and control every time. You can keep your eye on the goal when you don't have to keep looking back to see if the rest of the team is still behind you.

In subsequent positions where I had the power, I knew that there was a more effective way to lead. However, it does take more than leadership based on empowering and taking the advice of those closest to the action. It takes a leader who is genuinely interested in what's best for all to create a culture that is truly inclusive.

I used to tell everyone, "My job is to take the aggravation and yours is to do the work. If you promise to send the aggravation my way, I promise not to do a lick of work." It was my way of saying that my job was to do everything possible to create a climate where they could do their job. They all knew that I wouldn't ask them to do anything that I wasn't willing to do.

I learned that a leader must recognize the need to include all those involved. We all understand the need to keep our customer's interests in mind, but there are many others whose interests are vital to success. Our fellow workers are most important and so are their families. Our vendors and suppliers are important. Our communities are important. The environment is important. Keeping all those factors in mind and their best interest at heart takes a level of leadership that requires character and dedication.

Our son Bob, after working in a less than nurturing business climate for eight years, went out on his own. He later said that he had pretty much come to the conclusion that the business culture that he had seen in my companies and those his older brother and sister ran was fine for these smaller enterprises, but that larger national corporations like the one he had just left were too big for that kind of thing to work. Or so he thought. I guess I forgot to tell him about Heinz.

However, since he and his partners were starting out small, he decided to give it a try. Now he says he can't understand why anyone would do it any other way. Their customers cut them slack when they need it, their suppliers are understanding when they need a little time to pay, and their competitors respect them. His company gets repeat business because former customers know that Bob, his partners, and everyone on their team has the ability to deliver and that they take pride in their work. New customers are attracted by their reputation, the kind of reputation you build with an ethical business model.

Bob tries to never miss an employee's birthday, and he makes sure his people can put their families first. They know he cares about them and their families. He says, "I have found that the more ways you find to be there for your people, the more they will be there for you when you need them."

Even if you did not care a whit for your employees, customers, and suppliers, wouldn't you want the benefits that accrue from treating them all with respect? Satisfied customers, productive employees, happy suppliers, a community that respects you and is happy to have you in their midst — why would you want it any other way?

You don't have to be weaned on the ethical business model. You can choose to bring this trait into your life. You need only know that it works. This is not to say that being unprincipled never works, just that the potential for financial success is greater in a nurturing, ethical business climate than in the toxic barracuda atmosphere that exists in some workplaces. And while it may not sound like much, you will enjoy personal satisfaction even if you fail financially. Just think how crappy the bad guys feel when they fail, and they do, frequently, more frequently than the good guys.

Can you make everybody happy? Of course not. Employees will still take advantage of you. You will still have unreasonable customers and suppliers who rip you off or fail to deliver when you need them. But the alternative to doing the right thing by everyone you deal with is much less attractive. Because no matter how you rationalize it, even if you achieve great financial success, you will have a hole in your life.

Besides, if financial success is one of the things that might be nice, you have a better shot at getting there when you do the right thing. In the next four chapters I trace the history of the ethical business model. In part two I show some examples of the price businesses and others pay when they stray from this model. In part three I take a look as some of the companies that are taking the lead today in advancing the ethical business model. I hope to help you decide what kind of a company you want to lead or be a part of and, more important, what kind of life you would like to look back on. &

Live so that when your children think of
fairness and integrity, they think of you.
H. Jackson Brown, Jr.

CHAPTER TWO

IN THE BEGINNING

While our forefathers were bringing
democracy into the New World, Robert
Owen was bringing an ethical business
model into the industrial revolution.

Large business entities are a relatively new phenomenon. A little over two hundred years ago the industrial revolution was hitting its stride after a couple hundred years of fits and starts. England was staggering following the loss of their American Colonies. The French Revolution had monarchies all over Europe on edge.

In the latter part of the 1700s, commerce moved rapidly from home-based enterprises into the factories. For eons the family had been a self-sufficient productive unit. Their sheep provided wool and mutton. There was a cow, a pig, some chickens, a garden, and inside a humble home, a spinning wheel and a loom. And there was work, unending labor from dawn to dusk. Every member of the family was busy every waking hour just to squeak out a living.

In 1760 James Hargreaves's Spinning Jenny partially automated the cloth making process. A few years later Richard Arkwright invented what was called the Water Frame. Samuel Crompton combined their ideas into his Spinning Mule and moved cloth making out of the hands of the village artisans and into the mills. This automated machinery powered by water created an explosion of factories along waterways across England. By the turn of the century, it was all over. By 1800 the misery of home-based labor had been trumped by the utter despair of the mill and the tenement.

Those who adapted struggled, those who did not, starved. The owners soon filled their mills with children, some tiny tots as young as four or five, working twelve hours a day under unconscionable conditions. In 1771, Robert Owen was born into this changing world. He set off from his birthplace in Wales to go to London to learn the leather trade. He was just ten years old.

By the time he was twelve, he became a salesman for the firm. He had charm and a winning manner and soon moved on to a better sales position with a men's clothing establishment. After a time he offered to give up his salary and take only a commission. Within a year Owen had saved £100, a small fortune in that time. Just eighteen years old, he was ready to go into business for himself. He bought three of the new Spinning Mules and began turning raw cotton from the "New World" into cloth.

Within a year he had tripled his fortune, and at nineteen he made the acquaintance of a man with the Dickensesque name, Peter Drinkwater, who owned a large mill employing 500 in Manchester. Drinkwater purchased Robert Owen's equipment and goods and hired him at £300 a year to manage his mill. For six weeks Robert changed nothing, he just walked about the mill and got to know the employees. (I wonder if he was the model for HP, Peter Drucker, and Tom Peters.) Each day he was the first to arrive and the last to leave the mill.

Once he felt he knew what was needed, he began to act. He improved the working conditions, visited the workers in their homes, advising and helping as needed. He set up schools for those who worked in the mill and for the younger children at home. The first year he quadrupled Drinkwater's profit. When the owner came up from London to see what this young genius had done, he found a clean, tidy factory with happy, highly productive workers. He gave Owen a £100 bonus and a new contract with a percentage of the profits built in.

Now in his early twenties, Robert Owen kept improving the lot of his workers and Drinkwater's profits kept growing. He added windows and ventilation to the plant. He refused to hire very young children. When a Board of Health was established, he did not join the opposition group of mill operators but proudly invited the Board to come in and see what were, for that day and age, excellent working conditions.

Not only was the mill well run and extraordinarily profitable, the quality of the goods was the finest in the business. Owen's pride in his work led him to attach a label to each package of goods, declaring proudly: "These fine goods were made under the supervision of Robert Owen."

When Drinkwater wanted to buy out his contract so he could put his nephew in charge, Owen offered to cancel it at no charge. Drinkwater had no idea that when Owen left he took the most valuable asset of the company with him, his name, by now synonymous with quality goods.

Robert Owen had become a "brand." Soon he was acting as a broker for those mills that agreed to produce goods to his standards. They were allowed to place his mark of quality on them: "These fine goods were made under the supervision of Robert Owen."

At twenty-seven, while in Scotland, he met the charming daughter of a mill owner and bought her father out for £60,000. The mill was in a beautiful setting outside of Glasgow in a tiny community called New Lanark. Now with a mill of his own and the love of his life at his side, Robert Owen was ready to show what could be done by doing the right thing.

He reduced the workday from twelve to ten hours. He put in showers and provided healthy meals, often eating with his workers. Instead of tenements he built them comfortable cottages and offered prizes for the most beautiful gardens grown from flower seeds he provided. He banned the sale of alcohol in the village. Owen lived simply among his workers. Once when their supply of cotton was cut off for three months, he kept everyone on full pay and had them busy working to improve the community.

He built a combination nursery school, kindergarten, and grade school. It ran day and night caring for the small children of women who worked in the mill and teaching the older children and anyone else who wanted to learn. Those who worked in the school were not permitted to whip or hit the children; Owen explained that it only taught them violence. Makes you wonder if Dr. Spock knew about Robert Owen?

Owen sold stock to buy new equipment and improve the mill. He paid a 5% dividend to his new stockholders, a very good return for the time, and put every extra penny of profit into improving the lot of his workers. He believed that clean water, a sewage system, healthy employees, trees, and flowers were a benefit to everyone and the bottom line. And he had the bottom line numbers to prove it.

Soon dignitaries, business and political leaders, even heads of state came to New Lanark to see this miracle. But other mill owners, and — of all people— the clergy began to find fault. Because Owen refused to hire little children, parents across the land worried that this radical idea would spread and they would lose the income produced by their kids. He was accused of violating the right of fathers to profit from the labor of their children. Anyone can see the injustice in Owen's crazy ideas. Good grief!

His London stockholders began to grumble that his high-minded ideas were wasting their profits. They demanded that he either buy their stock —which they knew he was unable to do because he had ploughed his share of the profits back into the mill— or sell out to them. He was forced to sell.

Robert Owen was in his fifties. His now considerable fortune allowed him to travel widely. In 1825 he embarked on a speaking tour of the United States to talk about his experience in and the community that he built around his legendary mill. He spoke at town halls, universities, and to a joint session of the Congress. Owen had a private meeting with the President of the United States, John Quincy Adams.

His economic theories had intermingled with those of communal living, a growing movement in America and a precursor to socialism. He purchased a large commune in southern Indiana along the Ohio River. His plan was to bring cotton up the Mississippi and the Ohio by steamboat and create a great mill owned by the workers. Returning to England to tend to his growing interests there, he sent his twenty-five-year-old son, Robert Dale Owen, to America to oversee the enterprise, accompanied by several hundred of his followers.

The young man was soon overwhelmed by the problems inherent in this flawed social concept. His father had not done his homework. None of the other American communes survived more than two or three years, save those based on a religious community. And even those died out in time. Owen was not the first or the last to be beguiled by the seemingly reasonable proposition: "From each according to his ability, to each according to his need." His commune floundered and the people scattered within a year. All that remained —and remains today— is Owensboro, Kentucky, the village they founded across the river. Owen did not understand that a self-interest driven enterprise must include rewards for those who work harder.

Meanwhile, back in England, Owen paid off the debts of the experiment in America and divided up the assets, including the 30,000 acres of prime land he had acquired, among his children and, in his words, "a few of my staunch friends who have such a lavish and unwise faith in my wisdom."

Robert Owen lived out his long life promoting other enterprises that improved the lot of the people, particularly the workers. Among them, he created the first department store. Most of his family remained in the United States living on the land he gave them in southern Indiana.

Robert Dale Owen, the son who had headed the ill-fated experiment, was elected to represent the district in the Congress and later served as U. S. Ambassador to Italy.

As one of the first major factory owners to demonstrate that doing the right thing is the road to riches, Robert Owen is owed a debt by all who have followed. While his effort to take the concept to a level beyond the bounds of human nature was a failure, it certainly doesn't diminish the respect we owe this pioneer. The Drinkwater mill in Manchester and his mill in New Lanark were successful beyond anyone's expectations, except his. ∞

*I have always recognized that the object of
business is to make money in an honorable manner.
I have endeavored to remember that
the object of life is to do good.*
Peter Cooper

CHAPTER THREE

AN EDUCATED MAN
Peter Cooper instinctively built
ethics into everything he created.

The promise of America was emerging in 1791. The Bill of Rights was ratified and one of America's great citizens was born in New York City. Peter Cooper was the middle child of nine and his lot in life, like many a poor boy, was filled with ceaseless work and chores. He went to school for a few hours a day for less than a year, and grew to manhood hungry for learning.

He learned to build carriages and even as a teenager he devised easier and better ways to carry out his work. During his lifetime his inventions and resourceful nature led him from one successful endeavor to another.

He invented a steam engine that was a great improvement over the engine developed in England by James Watt. In 1828 the President handled patents, so Peter went down to Washington and showed his engine to John Quincy Adams, who gave him a patent.

He built the first steam locomotive in the United States and with it brought the Baltimore and Ohio Railroad into being. It was an act of resourceful desperation. Cooper had invested heavily in real estate and other ventures in and around Baltimore. When the Erie Canal made connecting the east and west easier, the overland route from Baltimore to Pittsburgh and the Ohio River was no longer competitive. The Port of Baltimore was dying and so was the city. Cooper faced massive losses.

Peter combined his carriage building skills with his steam engine. That led to the B&O and established a competitive rail connection to the Ohio River. The Port, Baltimore, and Cooper's investments were saved. He built a factory to make rails for this newfangled transportation. Cooper was the father of the railroad age that was the key to America's financial prosperity over the next century.

He was also the father of international electronic communications. As President of the New York, Newfoundland & London Telegraph Company, he steered the company as it connected the new world with the old in the mid-1800s by laying the first undersea cable across the Atlantic Ocean.

His ingenuity knew no bounds. He developed the first metal skeleton building decades before Louis Sullivan used that concept to create the first skyscrapers. Cooper had no such thought; he just had some surplus iron bars in one of his factories. Through an odd series of events he acquired a glue factory and was soon known for producing the finest glue available. Using a by-product from his glue factory and with the help of his wife, Sarah, he developed gelatin, the forerunner of Jell-O. This was not Sarah's only role in his business affairs. It was said that he discussed every idea and deal with her. She was his closest advisor and most trusted associate. Theirs was a true life partnership.

His reputation was built on more than the quality of his goods and services. He was known to conduct every aspect of his business based on fairness and honest dealings. In an era when Caveat Emptor (Let the buyer beware) was the rule, Peter Cooper took the high road in all his dealings. Then as now, doing the right thing and building a reputation as an honest businessman paid off. Peter Cooper became a very rich man, perhaps the richest in New York City at that time.

His idol was Benjamin Franklin, who died a year before Cooper was born. Cooper knew that, like him, Franklin had only one year of formal education. And like Franklin, Cooper felt the future of the country lay in educating its people. Franklin was turned off by what we now call the Ivy League Schools in his native New England. He felt they focused on the privileged in that day, ignoring the poor. Cooper shared this feeling and was determined to found an institution of higher learning that would serve the poor like Franklin and himself. In his sixties, Cooper began to build his school, The Cooper Union. And to be sure he got the school he wanted, he maintained total control: his money, his plan, his school.

He believed education should be "as free as water and air." From the very beginning the Cooper Union focused on providing opportunities in both traditional and non-traditional educational models. His genius and resourceful nature served him in planning his school. He offered night classes for adults, a precursor to modern day adult education. He encouraged both men and women to attend, offering special classes in "fashion" to be sure young women gained useful skills.

But the first thing he built was not a classroom. He built an auditorium, 900 seats in a horseshoe around a platform designed to attract the great minds of the world. An auditorium where common folk off the streets of New York could come to listen and to learn. When the college opened a year later, his hall had attracted some of the greatest names of the time to its platform. Abraham Lincoln gave his "Right Makes Might" speech from the Great Hall podium. Its fame continues. The Great Hall at the Cooper Union[4] is home to public forums, cultural events, and community activities.

And his dream continues. Cooper Union continues today as a full-scholarship, private college offering education for —as he put it— "the boys and girls of this city, who had no better opportunity than I."

Peter Cooper did the right thing! ❧

---

[4] Information on the Cooper Union is based in part on the institution's website: http://www.cooper.edu/administration/about/history.html

Necessity is the mother of invention.
Plato

CHAPTER FOUR

THE MOTHER OF INVENTION
To Jamie Oliver life was simple:
see a problem, find a solution.

About the time Robert Owen was leaving Scotland for America, James Oliver was born in that fabled land. Oliver was the youngest of eight. His father was content to scratch out a living tending another man's sheep. His mother, on the other hand, was determined to go to America. They finally made it and in 1836 found themselves in Mishawaka, just outside South Bend, Indiana. The state was giving anyone who would live and work on it a rich piece of fertile earth, a farm. A far cry from keeping someone else's sheep in the rocky hills of Scotland.

Jamie, as he was called, was a hard worker who loved farming till the day he died. But he found himself doing a lot of jobs, from working among the rough and tumble river men on the St. Joseph River to learning to smelt iron and make barrels.

He fell in love with a beautiful young woman for whose family he had done some odd jobs. She was far above his class and lived in one of the fanciest houses in town. When her father told him that he could not consider having his daughter marry unless her husband-to-be owned a house, Jamie found a nice one-room fixer-upper and bought it for $18. Daddy relented (mostly to please his darling daughter, I would judge) and they were married.

A few years later he ran across a fellow in South Bend who wanted to sell his interest in a less than successful foundry. Jamie had experience working iron and so he came up with the $88 the man wanted and went into business. A part of the business was making the one-horse plows that farmers relied on to turn the soil. Jamie Oliver knew from backbreaking personal experience that the plows of the day could stand considerable improvement.

He devoted several years to finding the right design and materials. The result was his "chilled plow," so named for his proprietary method of hardening the metal. He sold his first Oliver Chilled Plow in 1870. In just a few years his little foundry grew to a 30-acre industrial complex, the Oliver Chilled Plow Works, capable of producing a half-million plows a year. His innovative design reduced the effort of the horse by half, and of the man guiding the plow by at least that amount.

Through it all Jamie Oliver never saw himself as a factory owner or a businessman. He scorned finance. Bored by the endless proceedings, he frequently walked out of the meeting when his Board of Directors got into too many details. He saw himself as a farmer, solving problems for farmers. He saw his employees as vital to solving those problems and felt a responsibility to make their lives comfortable so they could concentrate on that task.

On more than one occasion when financial woes struck the nation, Oliver kept his plant producing, storing the plows his dealers could not sell until better times came. He never laid off workers and never reduced wages. He saw his employees as an asset, not a cost center. And they saw him as deserving their best effort and loyalty.

To put the importance of Oliver's ideas in perspective, remember that at the time, 60% of Americans lived on farms. He made the lives of those folks easier and more productive. He played a vital role in the largest sector of the economy of that day. Jamie Oliver considered himself a farmer, a friend of the farmer, a partner of the farmer, and a partner of nature. His success and his wealth came not from seeking it but from seeking solutions that would benefit his fellow men. Jamie Oliver saw a better plow as a necessity, and followed Plato's path. ∞

To do a common thing
uncommonly well
brings success.
H. J. Heinz

CHAPTER FIVE

MORAL DEBTS

H. J. Heinz was ahead of the
curve ethically, decades ahead.

The industrial revolution was in high gear in the late 1800s and no place on earth illustrates the extremes it created more than Pittsburgh, Pennsylvania. On one side stood Andrew Carnegie's huge steel mills. The gutsy little Scot built a huge steel enterprise largely on benevolent principles. But when his empire was threatened by hard times and falling steel prices, his resolve and moral fiber failed him.

The defining moment in his life came in 1892 at his Homestead Works. With Carnegie's full support, his plant manager, Henry Frick, imposed draconian wage reductions and declared that he would not negotiate with the workers' union. The union represented only a small fraction of the plant employees, but Frick's demands brought the vast majority of the workers to its defense. The union and the employees were willing to concede everything Frick wanted. But Frick wanted to kill the union, and that the workers inside and outside the union would not concede.

With Carnegie far away in Scotland, the pig-headed Frick locked the workers out, called in Pinkerton Agency's private army, and turned a solvable dispute into a war. The workers drove off the Pinkertons at the cost of a dozen lives. Then National Guard troops came in and drove the workers off. New workers were hired and the union was crushed. It's hard to imagine this outcome had Carnegie been there to see events unfolding. We know he came to regret his choices in this matter and it forever tarnished his legacy. All the libraries, a great university, and his other numerous charities could not erase the stain of his tacit approval of this pointless tragedy.

The lesson Carnegie gained in Homestead was not lost on another local business leader, Harry Heinz. After observing the outcome of a violent railroad strike fifteen years earlier, Heinz had been pursuing ways to immunize his business from violence by creating a working atmosphere that would make it, and labor unions for that matter, unnecessary.

In 1892 Heinz was expanding his food packing enterprise on the north shore of the Allegheny River in a community of the same name across the river from Pittsburgh. His factory was to grow larger and larger in the last decade of the nineteenth century. And as it grew it became a model for enlightened employee working conditions. Like Owen, Oliver, and a few others, Heinz was out of step with the conventional thinking of the day in every aspect of his business.

He began packing horseradish in his parents' basement. A talented promoter and salesman, he grew the business. But he ran aground and was forced into bankruptcy as a result of his out-of-touch-with-reality (as his competitors saw it) idea that preserving food intended for his fellow human beings should be done under sanitary conditions. He persisted, however, starting over again and even going back and paying off those who lost money when his earlier enterprise went bankrupt. He called those "moral debts."

He outraged his competitors when he supported and even lobbied in favor of federal laws to assure that food packers maintained sanitary conditions and that they refrained from the use of harmful preservatives. He became the most hated individual among his fellow food packers. Conversely, he was equally loved by his employees, suppliers, customers, and his community. A phrase that becomes a mantra in this book.

The H.J. Heinz plant that emerged as the century turned was unique in almost every way. It was bright and sparkling clean. A wide range of foods were preserved and packed by natural processes under pristine conditions. Those who worked in the plant (mostly women) wore clean blue and white uniforms and were required to maintain high standards of personal cleanliness. Every employee was given a weekly manicure.

Employees were offered a wide range of educational, recreational, and social opportunities. A roof garden and reading room were provided for use by the workers; a swimming pool, regular outings and picnics made it an ideal place to work. Far ahead of its time and not bad even by today's standards. Sounds almost like life at the Googleplex.

Much of my view of how a business should operate was drawn from my mother's experience as an employee at the H.J. Heinz Company in the early part of the twentieth century. She worked as a secretary, having achieved a then rare four-year high school education plus a business school degree. Her position was unusual since private secretaries in those days, especially those who served high-ranking executives, were almost always men.

She worked for Nevin Woodside, VP Sales and a member of the Heinz Board of Directors. Woodside and Heinz had offices side by side. Mom frequently did work for Mr. Heinz as well. Over many years with the firm, beginning just as America entered World War One, she observed these corporate leaders on a daily basis and understood their goal to run a company on the highest ethical standards.

Woodside was responsible for the Heinz advertising programs, perhaps the most aggressive of their time. Mother came away from her time at Heinz with a real appreciation of the value of their promotional efforts. They created the first large-scale electric sign in New York City. It was one hundred feet tall, covering the entire wall of a ten-story building at Fifth Avenue and 23rd Street.

Heinz's great success at several World's Fairs around the turn of the century led him to build a huge pier on the famed Atlantic City Beach in 1899. There were two large ornate buildings, one at the shoreline and an even larger one fifty yards out into the surf at the end of the pier. It was topped with a giant sign with the numerals 57 in bright lights. Both buildings were filled with curiosities and works of art. And of course, product samples and promotional materials featuring the company's products. Always looking for ways to put his people before the public, Heinz displayed large photos of his key employees including the district sales representatives. The Heinz Pier attracted millions over the 45 years it was open up to the end of World War II.

As the one who took her away from it all (in those days the arrival of a child was the end of a woman's working career), I was weaned on the business principles that Mother experienced at Heinz.

All this in a home that honored God and Organized Labor in that order and not too far apart. After two years of unemployment during the depression, Father finally found work as a bus driver. He loved driving. He got up every morning looking forward to seeing all the folks who rode his bus. And they looked forward to seeing him. More than once as a kid while standing at a bus stop I saw people pass an opportunity to board a bus, saying, "I'll wait for Mack's bus." He was known to turn down a side street on a rainy day to drop someone off in front of their house, and he took pride in never opening the bus door at a puddle or a snow bank.

Father was a union officer for all the years that I was growing up. So I heard the issues he was dealing with nightly at the supper table. The suburban bus line he worked for was owned by a corporate lawyer in Pittsburgh. Father believed him to be a good man who just did not realize the problems that his employees were dealing with. I gained an education in "what," as Father put it, "the men really want."

I later found that insight invaluable in creating a workplace atmosphere where the men and women I worked with could do their best. And I found, as did H. J. Heinz, that kind of atmosphere was the key to make labor conflicts unnecessary. More important, when people work in this kind of atmosphere, they produce more. That translates into both higher wages and more profit. That's what we now call a "win-win." ⋈

A business that makes nothing but money
is a poor kind of business.
Henry Ford

PART TWO

THE ALTERNATIVE
There have always been slow
learners. They usually pay the
price; unfortunately, not always.

Now that we have the idea that this is some kind of untested radical
new idea out of the way, let's examine the alternative. What happens
in the real world when you follow the dog-eat-dog school of business
management? Well, just like in the movies, sometimes you can crush
everyone in your way, claw your way to the top, and get very rich. More
often you get crushed and end up blaming your failure on somebody you
stepped on in your frantic climb before you fell off the ladder.

But win or lose, it's a hard road to follow. In this section of *Play Nice* I
am going to illustrate the price you may have to pay. I won't pretend
that you might not crash and burn if you follow the high road. If you
are to succeed in business, you have to be willing to take risks. To win
big you have to risk big. No matter what business model you follow,
one misstep and you can find yourself broke. Success is not possible
without the possibility of failure.

The premise of this book is to make clear that those who choose to do
the right thing in their business career, and businesses that are run on
that model, make more money. If you can attract a loyal and devoted
team, they are more likely to work hard to avoid fatal missteps. What's
more, it is likely they will make every effort to save a workplace they
find fulfilling and nurturing. It doesn't get any more logical than that.
But first let's examine some of what most often befalls those who buy
into business as a kill-or-be-killed proposition.

Let's say you do get rich by doing whatever you believe you have to,
clawing your way to the top and charging after every dollar. Just how
happy are you going to be? I have known many, many very rich people.
The money did not make any of them happy. Too often it brought them
—and even more so their children— unhappiness.

Money is only worth having if you don't care if you lose it. If it owns you, it is the cruelest of masters.

As my Dad, who never had more than enough money to barely get by, was wont to say, "I feel sorry for people who work for money." If that's all you get out of your workday, it's not much. He was always a Chevy guy, but in this case he would agree with Henry Ford.

Charles Dickens told this tale again and again in the setting of the cruel mid-1800s, never better than in his *Christmas Carol.* Scrooge found happiness only when he focused on the people he could help. If the race is just about the money, win or lose, there is no happiness at the finish line. That's a lose-lose scenario.

Even if you do the right thing, like H.J. Heinz you could go bankrupt, you may lose. But like Heinz you will find it a lot easier to pick yourself up and start over again. Even if you end up scraping by for the rest of your life, you will remember the satisfaction of running an honest race. You'll be able to look your children in the eye, and yourself in the mirror. Trust me, that's something no amount of money can buy.

In this part I take a look at some of those who bought into the hard-ass business model. They all paid a price. Although some came away with a lot of money I wouldn't trade places with any of them. More important, they all would likely have done much better if they had taken the high road. In those cases it would be Play Nice, Make <u>More</u> Money, and feel good. ☜

The Code is more what you'd call
'guidelines' than actual rules.
Geoffrey Rush as Captain Barbossa
Pirates of the Caribbean (2003)

CHAPTER SIX

THE CODE
Ethics policies on paper
are worthless if they are
not ingrained in the culture.

I have done a lot of public speaking. When I was in broadcasting back in the sixties, I used to throw out a question that always stumped the audience. What nation has the strongest constitutional protection for freedom of speech and freedom of the press? Of course the USA got most of the votes. The room would grow very quiet when I revealed the answer no one ever guessed: the Soviet Union, the dreaded Commies.

Given the era —at the height of the cold war, when every word spoken and written in Russia was controlled— it seemed an unlikely choice. But it was true. Actually, the simple statement in our Bill of Rights is among the shortest and least specific among all the nations on the planet. The point was then, and is now, that it doesn't matter what a nation or an organization says. It matters what they do.

Many companies have Ethics Codes, Policies, Statements, whatever, enough paper to fill a file cabinet. One of the most seemingly high-minded was the pride and joy of Enron CEO Kenneth Lay. He was forever going on about character. All the while overseeing a cynical batch of opportunistic schemes to manipulate energy prices.

Some of the best ethics policies are the shortest. Take Nordstrom, the department store folk with a reputation for exemplary customer service. Their employee handbook is business card size. It says: "One Rule: Use good judgment in all situations." That says it all for a principled company and in their case, like many others, it has paid off handsomely.

Enron, Tyco, WorldCom, Adelphia, and all the other recent scandals involve a variety of smarmy behavior that is more than unethical, it is illegal. And that brings us to a very delicate point, lawyers. Lawyers – as is the case with all disciplines– come in all shades of good and bad. Even the best, however, are rarely equipped to deal with ethics. Not because they are bad people; because they are trained to find the line between legal and illegal. As a code of ethics, that amounts to "It's OK if we can get away with it."

I've seen this tendency in play many times. Perhaps the most illogical was when it was applied by one of the most ethical individuals I have ever known. One of the clients in our public relations practice, a large publicly held firm, was headed by an individual who had risen into the CEO chair after years in private practice and serving as the company's General Counsel.

Shortly after we began working with them, it was discovered that a few of their outside sales people had been stealing from the company. The CEO conducted a thorough investigation and terminated several people. The worst offender by far happened to also be the most devious. Despite ample evidence that he was running a batch of kickback schemes, no solid proof could be documented.

The fact that he was also incompetent gave the company good reason to terminate him. However, the CEO's legal training would not allow him to dismiss the thief because the company did not have enough hard evidence. Because, in his own mind, he couldn't make a legal case against him, the CEO spared an individual who betrayed the company and his fellow workers. Usually it works the other way around. When lawyers get involved in ethical issues, it too often turns out bad.

Self-serving as it sounds, in my experience communications strategists make the best ethics officers. I know that some in our discipline are spin-doctors, charlatans. Many seem to think PR stands for Press Release and are unable to create anything beyond hyperbole. Spin Factories and Press Release Mills are, however, in the minority. Most pros know that doing the right thing is the only thing that works, and they are the first to sense that the company's reputation is at risk.

A couple years ago I wrote a piece for *Grasping Globalization*, my associate John Manzella's sixth book. This opportunity led me to put down on paper some principles that have guided me over the years. I call them my "Five Rules." They have been reprinted in a number of languages all over the world. They appeared in the leading U.S. public relations journal, the *Bulldog Reporter*. That began a relationship with that journal that ultimately led to this book. Here are my rules:

Five Rules That Will Protect You From Serious Harm, Even If Bad Luck Strikes

1) Do the right thing. Forget short-term results. Discard your ego. Long-term corporate health is based on fair dealings and a happy workforce. Happy employees will make your customers happy, and that combination will make your stockholders happy.

2) When you are forced to make tough decisions, be pro-active. Consult with those involved; see if they can find a way to lessen the impact. Be sure everyone knows what the choices are. Let your employees, the stockholders, the people in the affected communities, and your customers know what alternatives you are facing and what you must do.

3) Make the media your partner. Connect with them early on. Tell them everything as soon as those closest to the issues are on-board. Most journalists want to convey the truth. Candor and openness will be rewarded. If there are factors that will help the media understand an issue but would be better not published, ask if you can go off-the-record. If you establish an atmosphere of trust, you can work with the media and they will work with you.

4) If something bad happens, get it out immediately. This is always the hardest part of dealing with the media. If you attempt to hide anything or hold back, the media will speculate, rumor will become fact. Instead of one day or one week of bad press, the media will quite properly keep probing and it will drag on and on. The classic case is the 1982 Tylenol poisoning tragedy. Johnson & Johnson did the right thing. And while that isn't why they did it, it paid off.

Faced with seven deaths, Johnson & Johnson halted sales and recalled 31 million packages of the product worth more than $100 million. They initiated an internal investigation that showed conclusively that the poison was added after the product left their control. They offered a reward for capture of the perpetrator and came to the aid of the grieving families of the victims. In quickly aligning themselves with the victims and getting the facts out, they showed that they were victims as well.

Prior to the poisonings, Tylenol had 37% of the over-the-counter pain medication market, three times its nearest competitor. Their response was so successful that they regained that position in little more than a year. Compare this outcome with the public relations catastrophes at Three Mile Island and Perrier.

5) "Hire the best lawyers you can find, but never allow them to make a decision." In his autobiography, Confessions of an SOB, *former Gannett CEO and founder of USA* Today, *Allen Neuharth, lays out this business principle that is doubly applicable to public relations.*

A classic example of this rule is the Love Canal disaster in Niagara Falls, New York. The Hooker Chemical Company, owner of the toxic waste facility, was pressured to sell it to the local school district. The initial reaction of the company's executives was to resist. Their legal counsel advised against that course, suggesting instead that they draw up agreements that would absolve the company of any future problems and avoid a long eminent domain fight to keep control of the property. So they drew up the papers and sold the property.

Had they ignored this bad advice (see rule #1, "Do the right thing"), untold grief and a financial and public relations nightmare would have been averted. The Love Canal would have remained the well-protected waste dump it was before Hooker relinquished control over its future to those who ignored the danger that disturbing it entailed. And most of us would be unfamiliar with the name, Love Canal.[5]

The next few chapters examine others —some pretty good companies— who broke these rules and paid a price for that mistake. ❧

---

[5] Five Rules first appeared in *Grasping Globalization*, John Manzella, ©2005.

*To see what is right and not to do
it is want of courage.*
Confucius

CHAPTER SEVEN

LACK OF VISION
When leaders lack the courage to do the
right thing, they risk losing everything.

Otherwise trustworthy organizations always get themselves deeper into
trouble when they give a problem legs by pretending it doesn't exist. In
late 2005 reports connecting a contact lens solution produced by Bausch
& Lomb and cases of an eye infection began to surface. It was well into
2006 before B&L began to address the issue and even then they bobbled
their response.

In late August the *Bulldog Reporter* based a piece on a Rochester, New
York (their hometown), newspaper story in which Bausch & Lomb was
declared "off the hook." My OPED followed in their "Barks & Bites"
column the next week.

Swallowing the Hook!

*If Bausch & Lomb thinks they are "Off the Hook," they are either
delusional or whistling through the graveyard. The Federal Centers
for Disease Control conclusions published in the Journal of the
American Medical Association are far from giving them any
"reputation victory." Even their hometown newspaper piece quoted
does not help that much. As the Bulldog Reporter indicated, while the
CDC did not find any contaminants in B&L's production facilities,
they did conclude that the outbreak of eye infections centered on users
of two B&L products "may have contributed" to fungal infection in
certain instances due to their unique properties.*

*The major conclusion of the CDC study, according to its chief author,
is to confirm that contact lens wearers should not use ReNu with
MoistureLoc. B&L officials themselves previously highlighted
MoistureLoc's formula as a potential problem, especially in instances
when consumers fail to follow prescribed hygiene practices.*

And in those last eleven words lie the pitfall that has perhaps irreparably damaged Bausch & Lomb. Blame it on the victim. Even if that were the case –and the CDC clearly does not lean in that direction– it's a dumb response. It led to an inexcusable delay in issuing a recall. While B&L fiddled for months, their brand was being stomped into the ground.

There is one and only one inescapable rule when a product goes sour in the marketplace. At the first hint of a problem, recall the product. A rule that is doubly important when the public health is concerned. In this case a disease, Fusarium, that can cause a range of problems including blindness. Don't listen to the lawyers, don't listen to the bean counters, don't wait for internal investigations, run– do not walk– to your logistics people and stop all shipments. Have your marketing people contact every customer and pull the product off the shelves.

Call in the media. Tell them everything you know and everything you are doing. Offer refunds to consumers for product they return to your retailers. Urge people who suspect that they have symptoms to seek medical treatment. Offer to pay for treatment. In this case, there were only a couple hundred cases of Fusarium worldwide.

It's not just a case of saving your bacon; it's about doing the right thing. How could a company built on improving vision hesitate when there is a suspicion that one of their products could be causing eye damage? What could be worse? No one is saying B&L set out to hurt anyone. They simply did not act when they first knew there could be a problem.

They issued a series of statements cautioning users but did not do a recall until May 2006. When did they know they had a problem? Even if they didn't have a hint until they issued the first cautions in early 2006, they still waited months to do what they should have done minutes after the alarms started going off. Tracking the press releases posted on their website on this subject is a study in denial.

Tragically they apparently had the key to redemption at hand. According to Ben Rand's piece in the Rochester Democrat and Chronicle, "In a statement issued Tuesday [August 22, 2006], the company said the CDC's study would be helpful in developing new solutions."

If history (read Johnson & Johnson, Chicago, 1982) teaches our discipline anything, it teaches us what to do in this kind of situation regardless of motivation, self-interest or genuine regard for the public. If B&L's Chairman and CEO, Ronald Zarrella, had ordered the actions recommended above and gone to the media immediately, his company would be on the road to recovery today instead of reacting to more bad press.

He could have used what they learned about "developing new solutions" to create new products and be restoring the $100 million a year the product associated with Fusarium contributed to their sales. Instead, he is facing lost business and a host of trial lawyers. More important, his company could truly lay claim to the phrase they offer at every opportunity: "Bausch & Lomb is the eye health company, dedicated to perfecting vision and enhancing life for consumers around the world."
Reprinted with permission of the Bulldog Reporter's Daily 'Dog. Copyright 2006 by Infocom Group.

Things continued to worsen. The FDA came out and slapped B&L hard. And there are enough barracuda lawyers trolling for Fusarium victims to fill a ballroom. Bausch & Lomb faces a loss of brand image and a horrific legal battle that will drag on for years. It will distract them from moving the company ahead and will have a huge negative impact on their bottom line.

Standard & Poor's has downgraded its rating on Bausch & Lomb's debt to junk bond level. S&P also indicated that it may cut the rating further. Ultimately the mishandling of this tragedy led to a move to sell out to private equity firm Warburg Pincus. Taking the company private will pull it out of the public eye and doubtless lead to dramatic changes, probably beginning at the top.

Although that won't be too bad for CEO Ron Zarrella. Despite near criminal mishandling of the contact lens recall and close to a halving in earnings between 2004 and 2006, along with accounting scandals, our boy Ronnie covered himself with gold on the way into the job. Kicking him out will cost Bausch & Lomb a minimum of $40 million. He has a contract clause that makes getting fired almost something to wish for.

Compare that to another executive who took over a Rochester, New York, company in earlier days. When Al Neuharth took over a newspaper chain, Gannett, in that fair city, its revenues were about $165 million a year.

When he retired it was a dominant force in media, with over $3 billion in revenues. Neuharth asked his board to reward him for his success as well as others had been rewarded for failure. He was given a little over $5 million in 1989. Too bad Al didn't have the kind of package Zarrella negotiated that may give him eight times that much for catastrophic failure.

What happened to Bausch & Lomb can happen to anybody. Anyone can have an unintentional mishap with a product. And when it does it will hurt you. The impact can be softened, however, if you move quickly to minimize the damage and treat the victims with the compassion they deserve. Wouldn't you help a little old lady you knocked down on the street? How could you do any less for a customer harmed by your product?

Ironically, Ronald Zarrella's predecessor at B&L, Bill Carpenter, was at Johnson & Johnson when the Tylenol crisis hit. While that situation was different in that J&J was not at fault, they didn't know that when they reacted to the news that their product was killing people. Makes you wonder how Carpenter would have handled the B&L crisis?

It would be hard to find a better example of how ethical behavior would have had a positive effect on the bottom line of a company. By thinking of their bottom line first, Bausch & Lomb got the exact opposite of what they hoped for, a financial disaster. And a human disaster; they'll never be able to look themselves in the mirror again without thinking of those they injured in a heartless attempt to save a few dollars.

How different things would be today for B&L if they had pulled the product off the market the instant the first reports came in. If they had rushed to the aid of those injured and seen to it that they had the best medical care available. It would have reduced the number of victims. It would have given the barracuda bar less to work with and reduced their legal costs. If they had played nice when common decency was screaming for them to do so, money would have been the least of their savings. ࢷ

Ethics is knowing the difference between what
you have a right to do and what is right to do.
Potter Stewart

CHAPTER EIGHT

THE BARROOM BRAWL

A deadly brew of egos
and legal mentality
would make this funny
if it weren't so serious.

It is really sad when a great company shoots itself in the foot and then can't seem to get out of its own way, stumbling along into one mess after another. Hewlett-Packard is one of the great American success stories and is a great company. Hard-charging Carly Fiorina headed HP from 1999 through early 2005, when the board eased her out the door with a $21 million golden parachute. HP stock jumped 7%. Wall Street clearly was glad to see her go. As were many HP employees.

She was replaced as CEO by Mark Hurd with a more collaborative management style. Early in 2006, while he was bringing the company back into the kind of culture that made it great as well as producing maximum operating effectiveness and profitability, a catfight was breaking out in the boardroom. Someone on the board leaked word of the brawl to the media.

Board Chair Patricia Dunn, who took over that seat from Ms. Fiorina, had a hissy-fit and vowed to find the traitor. Instead of deliberating on corporate strategy, the HP Board divided its time between brawling and trying to locate the leak. The search for the culprit was turned over to some smarmy types who used questionable means to track him down. The whole operation was headed by HP's ethics officer, a lawyer, who reported to the company's General Counsel.

With that chain of command you know it had to turn out bad. In this case they failed even to find the legal line in the sand. The courts will decide in the end how many of the players inside and outside the company were on the wrong side of the law. Ms. Dunn, who has a journalism degree, should have known better.

Mark Hurd apparently was too busy to notice that the kids in the boardroom sandbox were not playing well together, but there is no indication that he was involved in any way. When the wheels fell off, Hurd issued a statement saying that they would "fix it." In September I offered him some suggestions in an OPED in the *Bulldog Reporter's* "Barks & Bites." Not surprisingly, in the unlikely event that he ever saw my thoughts, he ignored them. Instead he put the company back into compliance (legal) mode instead of ethics mode.

Fixing Hewlett-Packard

"This is just a horrible thing that has happened and we have to fix it." Those are the words of Mark Hurd, CEO of tech giant Hewlett-Packard. When the story broke on HP's ham-handed response to boardroom leaks, it wasn't hard to understand how the wheels came off. The hunt for the source was overseen by since-sacked Kevin Hunsaker, HP's Director of Ethics. Hunsaker is a lawyer; worse, he reported to the company's General Counsel.

Understand, lawyers are important and despite all the jokes, most of them like most of us are honorable folk. The discipline, however, is based on law, not ethics. Lawyers are trained to delineate the letter of the law. A necessary and worthy service to our society.

No one will likely ever know what really happened. We know that the hunt spiraled out of control, resulting in Ms. Dunn along with several members of the board and HP employees being ousted. Ironically Ms. Dunn has a BA from the UC Berkeley "J" school. Makes you wonder what she was thinking when she turned a pack of private eyes loose on the HP Board, employees and ultimately a number of journalists. In her defense there is no proof that Ms. Dunn OK'ed —or even knew about— the smarmy tactics that were used to track down the leak.

It's far from over, with the authorities in California looking into criminal charges. Those legal details are not our concern. And they wouldn't have been anyone's concern had ethics, rather than the letter of the law, guided their thinking. No one is quite sure why CEO Hurd was not aware of the means employed by those involved in the hunt. But if he wants to fix it, there is a simple answer. He needs a Director of Ethics empowered to act as the company conscience. A DOE reports only to the CEO and has a contract that makes them fearless, with a golden parachute that allows them to stand for the right thing no matter what.

The sad thing is that this whole mess is about petty bickering on the HP Board that would be embarrassing if it happened in a neighborhood pub. In a $3 billion company it is pathetic.
Reprinted with permission of the Bulldog Reporter's Daily 'Dog. Copyright 2006 by Infocom Group.

We know more now, and one thing we know is that my advice was ignored. Not that I expected them to pay any attention, but you would think that anyone as smart as Mark Hurd would figure out for himself what happened. But no, he first hires a fancy lawyer to fill in. Then he brings in another lawyer to head ethics. The good news: he will report to Hurd. Hold the presses, the bad news is: that's only temporary; he will report to Hurd until they get a new General Counsel and then it's back to the same old sure-to-fail-when-it's-most-needed model.

A year later, in May of 2007, HP is still in "compliance" mode and still slogging along. The S.E.C. slapped them again for smoothing over the reason why a member of their Board of Directors resigned in the midst of the catfight. Bloomberg News reports, *"The S.E.C. issued a cease-and-desist order against the company, requiring it to refrain from violating disclosure laws, and said that Hewlett-Packard agreed to the measure without admitting or denying wrongdoing."*

The last five words say it all. They not only did wrong, they did stupid. Mark Hurd should have issued a statement saying that they made a mistake and that it won't happen again. By letting the lawyers convince him to go along with the *"without admitting or denying wrongdoing"* legalspeak, Hurd tells his investors, customers, and the media that the company is more concerned about what they can get away with than what's right.

Albert Einstein put it, "We can't solve problems with the same thinking we used when we created them."

Only time will tell if HP will be burned again by this flawed approach to ethics. That, however, is not the central lesson that we glean from this tragic tale. Focus on the changing of the guard. Hurd's management style is not only a lot more benevolent, it is much more effective. Sales, profits, and their stock prices are all up. Too bad the brawling board of directors turned the continuing focus to their juvenile behavior. ॐ

> *When you throw out integrity,*
> *the rest is easy.*
> Larry Hagman as J.R. Ewing
> "Dallas" - CBS TV

CHAPTER NINE

THE SIREN SONG

Few set out to do wrong, but the first step often leads to another and then another and soon your compass and your soul are lost.

We have all been tempted to take a turn onto some path that doesn't appear to be "really" all that bad. But once you leave the straight and narrow, you soon find yourself in a dark place. A place where you are scrambling to remember what you said last. A place where each step takes you deeper into the mire. A place where you keep telling yourself that it's what you have to do in this world to "make it."

Take John Rigas, the deposed founder of cable giant Adelphia. As I write he awaits his fate while the appeals work their way through the courts. The likely outcome? Rigas will have little to do but review how differently things might have turned out had he followed the straight and narrow. He stands convicted of securities fraud; chances are he will spend his last few years on earth in jail.

How did this seemingly warm, beloved example of the small town Horatio Alger success story end up in this position? Rigas was the very picture of a business leader who seemed dedicated to doing the right thing. Had I been writing this book ten years ago, Adelphia might have been one of my poster child examples of a contemporary company built on an ethical business model.

Is he a really bad guy or, as some think, an innocent led astray by others, primarily a trusted son? Since none of us can see into his heart, we may never know. But it's pretty hard to imagine that he was unaware of the massive financial shenanigans that went on at Adelphia for decades. And now as we are looking a little closer at his past dealings, there is evidence that Rigas personally pushed the limits from the day he set out to build his empire.

John Rigas, the overachieving first child of Greek immigrants, combined smarts and a willingness to take big risks for big rewards to parlay the ownership of a barely profitable theater in the tiny community of Coudersport, Pennsylvania, into one of the largest cable television empires in the world. Like most great success stories, there was more than a little good fortune involved. He was quite literally in the right place at the right time.

Coudersport is located where the New York and Pennsylvania border cuts through very hilly terrain. In the early days of television, reception there was worse than spotty. Back then cable was the only way folks who lived in that kind of terrain could get a decent signal and a choice of stations to watch, albeit no more than three or four. Cable operators started building antennas on the hilltops to pull in signals from the nearest stations and feed them to their customers.

During the fifties and sixties the cable industry was totally focused on remote rural areas and big cities, both locales difficult to penetrate with the broadcast technology existent. During that time John Rigas borrowed heavily to expand his empire and bought up neighboring cable systems right and left.

In the mid-sixties I was at WBEN-TV, the CBS affiliate in Buffalo, New York. These pioneer cable companies, including Adelphia, broadened our coverage immensely. A piece of research I commissioned back then showed that more than half the cable subscribers in the United States were stretched along a sixty-mile-wide east/west strip divided by the New York/Pennsylvania border. Rigas was literally in the middle of the Cable Promised Land.

Was he ever the benevolent, gray-haired good guy that his carefully crafted image conveyed, and if so, when did he turn to the dark side that led to his current status as a convicted felon? While we may never know, it clearly got totally out of hand when Adelphia went from being a private company owned by Rigas and his family to a public company with shares trading on the stock market and bonds in the money market. There are, however, indications that John played fast and loose with facts and numbers in their financial dealings from the day he went into business. At the very least, John Rigas displayed severe "Other People's Money Syndrome" throughout his business career.

What may be legal and even ethical in a company that you own, is a very different matter in a publicly held company. While that would seem to be abundantly obvious to most, the Rigas family seems to have —"wink, wink"— missed it. Want to buy a boat? Want to build a golf course just for you and your buddies? Want to fly a friend in the company jet? Private company, it's probably no problem to have the company pay for it, so long as you declare the value as income and pay the taxes. Public company, it's likely OK if your board of directors approves and you pay the applicable taxes. It was the latter rather simple line in the sand that the Rigas crew blatantly ignored. And once across that line, they went head first into the deep dark land of deceit.

The Rigas family has been widely pilloried for using Adelphia as a private "piggy bank." As time went on their dipping into the company till became outrageous. John's three sons were all part of the business, frequently identified in company boilerplate as, "each contributing their unique skills to the organization." It would seem those skills were grounded in greed. One observer noted wryly that John gave his sons the best education money could buy and they learned to steal big-time.

While that may be a bit harsh in the case of the eldest and youngest Rigas sons, it seems vastly understated in the case of the middle son, Tim. He was convicted of securities fraud and got a slap-on-the-wrist twenty-year prison sentence. Rumors have made him out to be a really nasty guy. His older brother, Michael, was acquitted. Insiders label him as clueless. Same for the youngest of the three brothers, James, who was not charged. All four members of the family face civil suits, however, that will likely strip them of everything but the clothes on their backs.

Indications are that while the "private piggy bank" allegations were true and that the Rigas family was into it big-time, that was just the tip of the iceberg. It was so outlandish and in some cases bizarre, that the really serious abuse got buried. The media had a lot of fun with the piggy bank stuff, while the big-time hanky-panky that actually sank the company seemed to go unnoticed. Adelphia was a huge company. Didn't it occur to the hot shot financial media types that while it was wrong, the piggy bank stuff wasn't anywhere near big enough to sink the company? If it crossed anyone's mind in the media, I missed seeing it.

So what was lurking under the waves that really sank the Good Ship Adelphia? Book cooking at unimaginable levels. They overstated profits by hundreds of millions a year, year after year after year. One of the tricks was to book common expense items as capital investments. A dumb move because it simply pushes expenses into future years and the deceit into a death spiral. To add to the problem they hung massive debt for business assets they held outside the public company on Adelphia, debt that was covered by bogus or no collateral, leaving stockholders holding the bag, an empty bag.

The media shouldn't feel too bad about missing the important stuff, since the federal prosecutors missed it too. One wonders if that was incompetence or grandstanding? Were they hoping to catch the headlines and make a career on the more outlandish moves of the arrogant thieves at the helm of Adelphia?

And then you wonder how the Rigas crew thought they could get away with it? Perhaps because they had been getting away with it for decades. And as they followed the song of the siren, each step seemed easier than the last.

The siren's melody does not necessarily lead individuals just into unlawful behavior. It can turn some from good folks into self-absorbed tyrants. One case that I witnessed from nearby, but not within, is the perfect example.

A bright young guy had the good fortune to find himself in an emerging industry rising quickly into management. At his right arm was another bright up-and-comer. The two of them made their way up the ladder together, actually building both the ladder and much of the industry as they went. They created one breakthrough concept after another. The money poured in and ownership showered them with cash and stock options.

Handsome and charming, they both married beautiful women. The lead dog married a movie star, his partner his college sweetheart. They parted company still friends a few years after they hit the top of the ladder. The lead dog stayed to head the organization they had created, his associate moved on to other green pastures. It was at this point that I was close enough to track their careers. I never got to know or even meet the lead dog, but while we never worked together, his associate became a close business friend.

In time the lead dog began, as the saying goes, to believe his own press notices. He was soon more feared than admired. While the company continued to do well in a climate where everyone in the industry was doing well, he was no longer hitting home runs every time he stepped up to the plate.

Worse, his behavior turned bizarre. His treatment of those he worked with no longer engendered loyalty. Everyone was too busy watching their back to do the kind of stellar work that had marked his leadership during the company's rise. The lead dog dumped his movie star wife and his personal life turned smarmy. He didn't break any laws that I know of, he just forgot where he came from, who he was, and how he had built the company. It was no longer a fun or even a great place to work and so great things no longer happened. He was fired. Not a big deal personally, since his stock options had made him a very wealthy man.

Not long after his very public exit, I was invited to dinner at the Manhattan home of his former associate. When the talk turned to the top dog I asked, "What was he like? You started out with him and the two of you worked side by side for years. What kind of a guy turns into this kind of person?"

There was a long pause. My friend's wife smiled and replied in her soft southern accent, "Funny you should ask. We were talking about that before you arrived. He was a bright, caring guy. We were just saying that he was a lot like you." It was a humbling conversation. I never caught the tail of a comet like the top dog, so great temptation was never placed in my path. But I never forgot that conversation, and I never stopped looking in the mirror to be sure that no trace of the top dog was beginning to emerge along with my modest successes.

The top dog shaped an industry. He helped to build a company that did great things and made a lot of money. He created a culture that was the envy of the industry. He did the right thing and success and money followed. Then somewhere along the way he lost his compass. And instead of the great leadership legacy that marked most of his life, he is remembered as a tyrannical jerk. ❧

> *It is not what a lawyer tells me I may do,*
> *but what humanity, reason, and justice*
> *tell me I ought to do.*
> Edmund Burke

CHAPTER TEN

MARTHA MUFFS IT
A little greed costs an icon
a lot more than a few bucks.

The price you pay when something goes awry is based on how you handle it. And how you handle it is based on the ethical model you build your life and your business on. No one but Martha Stewart knows if she really used insider information to dump some stock when it was about to go into free fall at the end of 2001. But let's take her at her word and say she was just following a long-established plan to sell if the stock dropped below a certain level. When the stock collapsed the day after she dumped all her shares, she had to know it might look like she had acted on inside information from the company's CEO. It was widely known that he and Martha were personal friends. It seems to me that a person in this situation who was following an ethical business model would have been horrified. As an innocent victim of timing, they would focus on making it right.

At that moment all that was at stake was the difference in value of her stock when she dumped it and what it would have been worth the next day when everyone learned about the company's problem. My rough calculations make that to be about $50,000. Now for most of us, that's a whole lot of money. For Martha Stewart it's a hit, but nothing that's going to make an impact on her lifestyle. She is a multi-millionaire with a huge media empire and valuable merchandise deals. But that's not the point. You just don't do these things if your goal is to do the right thing. No matter that it's illegal, it's not right to use inside information that other stockholders don't have. An ethical person would be more worried about their reputation than any legal issues or money losses.

So what was the right thing the day after she innocently sold her shares and found herself watching the stock go down, down, down? How about doing the math and saying, "Golly gee, I don't want this to look like I had any advance information, it would tarnish my reputation. I am going to give the $50,000 that I saved by selling yesterday to charity.

In fact, I'll double it and hand out $100,000. While it's obvious that I had no inside knowledge, I don't want there to be any doubt or reason to suspect otherwise." That would have been doing the right thing. It would have been over. To me her failure to react as any ethical person would is the most damning evidence against her. She hung tough and maintained that she had done no wrong. In the end it cost her a ton of money in legal fees and a trip to the slammer. Dumb!

There is another possibility. What would someone operating on an ethical business model have done if they did have inside information that they knew was going to cause a stock to lose some of its value? They would have done the right thing and held the stock. And how would that have worked out? Well, if they sold the next day they would have lost some money. As it turned out in Martha's case, the problem that caused the stock to collapse was resolved in favor of the company. Doing the right thing and holding the stock would have eventually paid off. Play Nice, Make Money.

Ms. Stewart comes across as a tough individual. Nothing in the media reports would indicate that "nice" is in her playbook. And while she has made a ton of money, we wonder how different her life might have been if she had applied her considerable talents to a more benevolent business model? Imagine all the people and organizations she could have had supporting her when things went wrong instead of worrying about triggering her displeasure. Imagine how much more money she would have made had those around her been free to focus on the good of the enterprise. Obviously she doesn't need any more money, but if she had chosen to Play Nice, she wouldn't have been focused on the money anyway, would she now? ∾

Everybody makes honest mistakes,
but there's no such thing as an honest cover-up.
Price Pritchett

CHAPTER ELEVEN

NOW FOR SOMETHING REALLY BAD
When management fails,
too often the innocent suffer.

No one expects stellar management skills in government. Neither party has a clue. But we should be able to expect a little common sense in serious situations. It would be hard to imagine a more serious situation than the one that faced the United States House of Representatives in 2006 when Representative Mark Foley was finally outed as a common pedophile.

While to some this looks like a political issue, on closer examination it is clearly a management issue. Those supervising Foley did not do their job. The "Beltway" culture ensnares even the media, who are charged with watching out for the interests of the citizens by keeping an eye on those we elect and send to the Congress. Everyone turned a blind eye to the abhorrent behavior of this monster. There were many reasons, but the bottom line is management failure. A failure in the most basic management responsibility, protecting the most vulnerable members of the organization.

Charged with caring for the teens who come to Washington to serve as pages, Foley instead used his position of trust to molest them. Those who want to make this just a Republican issue have got to be kidding. Foley's predatory behavior went on for at least the better part of a decade. That puts it directly under the noses of the members of two presidential administrations. There is no way that it was a secret. Lots of people had to know about it. They were not all Republicans. They were not all members of the Congress. Hosts of insiders, bureaucrats, congressional staffers, those in the White House, and of all people, members of the media heard the rumors, didn't check them out, did nothing. Tragically, even when the story finally came out, nothing happened! Foley was allowed to escape, unpunished. The leadership allowed him to resign taking himself beyond their ability to discipline him. He is free to find a new venue and prey on more children.

Here's what I had to say about it in the *Bulldog Reporter* after the House Ethics Committee whitewashed the incident in January of 2007.

Foley Follies

Last week's report from the House Ethics Committee of the U.S. Congress is beyond outrageous. They concluded that the members of the House who knew of the wildly improper sexual pursuit of teenage pages by Representative Mark Foley were "negligent," but they broke no "rules."

This bipartisan panel of two Republicans and two Democrats spent two months interviewing individuals and reviewing evidence. They put together a 91-page report that shows inexcusable lapses of common sense, decency, and a total disregard for the children entrusted to their care. And not by a few, but by dozens of those in positions of power. And not for a short period of time. Some individuals knew what Foley was up to for nearly a decade.

The only thing worse is the spin Republican apologists are putting on the affair. Their pitch is that Foley is just another Gay Guy, and that if he were a Democrat no one would think anything of it. There are a host of things wrong with that argument. Anyone —no matter their sexual orientation— who exhibits sexually inappropriate behavior when they are in a position of power, has crossed the line. Gay or straight, it is flat out wrong, and in many cases criminal.

Mark Foley is not just another Gay Guy. Mark Foley is a pedophile. His targets were teenage kids. Children entrusted to our highest legislative branch. These kids were there to learn how our government works. Instead they learned that sexual predators were free to attack them, protected by what the House Ethics Committee Report allows were "political considerations."

The contention that Foley's behavior resulted from alcoholism is an insult to drunks. Impaired driving skills are one thing; pounding on the door of the official House Page residence in the middle of the night is a totally different matter.

According to the report, House Speaker Dennis Hastert's chief counsel had been aware of Foley's behavior for "nearly a decade." It is hard to imagine that behavior this bizarre could go on for years without a lot of people, both Republicans and Democrats, knowing about it. It sounds like there was a bipartisan effort to turn a blind eye to this monster.

For those of us who deal with information, the lesson is simple. There are at least a couple levels of right and wrong. There is the legal line. A line the House Ethics Committee felt was not crossed by those who knew they had a serial pedophile among their brethren. And there is the ethical line. A line well above what you can get away with without violating the law. It is obvious that many, many people in and around the Congress went way beyond that ethical line.

No one knows better than we how things can spiral out of control once you step past that ethical line onto the clichéd slippery slope. Think how much better it would have been had someone exposed Foley the first time he got out of line. Think how much better it would have been for all the children he damaged. Think of how much better it would have been for the Congress. Think how much better it would have been even for Foley.

CEOs and others in carpet land are often occupied with other things. Accountants and lawyers are trained to look for the legal line. We [Public Relations and Corporate Communications types] are the front line troops when it comes to ethics. If it will cost you your job to sound the alarm, you are working for the wrong people. Ethics are the foundation of profitability and the only job security.

What went wrong in the Congress was clearly a management matter. The managers in the Congress failed to act when they should have. The same kind of denial that too often prompts business leaders to ignore signs of serious trouble led the managers in Congress to stick their heads in the sand. Then when it began to unravel, they tried to cover their tracks.

Underlings were afraid to blow the whistle in a working climate that does not encourage candor. The handwriting on the wall doesn't take a Daniel to read it.[6] This is a prime example of the need for my rule #4 in chapter 6: *When something bad happens, get it out quick. Take your licks; show that you have taken steps to correct the situation.* Anything less than instantaneous candor will only worsen the situation.

Actually, I learned this lesson first in the military. I was working in the base public information office when an incident caught the attention of one of the nation's leading newspapers. A reporter called the base and somehow was connected to a high-ranking officer on the headquarters staff. After telling the reporter half the story, the officer got cold feet and refused to answer any more questions.

The reporter quite naturally assumed that there was some deep dark secret involved and his story lambasted our command. When we called him and gave him all the rest of the facts, it was too late. He didn't believe us. He was sure we were hiding something. For weeks the paper slammed us on the front page and in blistering editorials. They put together some wild speculative scenarios in an attempt to flush out more information.

Finally they sent the reporter to visit the base. I met him at the airport and drove him the thirty or so miles to the base. It gave us the better part of an hour together. I answered his questions candidly and honestly. After a few minutes the talk turned to his experiences in combat as a war correspondent. He was a top-flight journalist who had seen it all.

We had been advised that he would be with us "as long as it took to get to the truth of the matter." So when we arrived at the base I took him to the guest quarters and handed him a map of the base, the keys to the staff car, and a card authorizing him to use the officers' club for meals. I explained that his newspaper would be billed for his stay including meals and mileage, so that there would be no suggestion that we were trying to influence him in any way.

I gave him a copy of an order from the commanding general to all personnel. It stated in no uncertain terms that the reporter was to be given access to all areas of the base, that all files were to be made

[6] Daniel 5:1-31

available to him, and that all personnel, military and civilian, were to answer his questions directly and truthfully. Finally, I gave him my phone number and headed out across the parade ground to the office.

Two hours later he called. He said he was ready to go back to the airport. After we pulled out he said something to this effect, "You've got to be telling the truth about this incident. You could get a few people to cover it up, but you could never get all the personnel —the thousands on this base— on the same page. What the hell was that colonel I talked to in headquarters thinking of when he clammed up on me the day this story broke? This could have been over that day if he had just had the sense to finish the story."

I wish I could say I devised that plan. I did not. It was devised by my boss, Major Nelson Bryant, a reservist, a brilliant magazine editor called back to active service. He knew that candor was the right thing to do and that a green kid like me with just a couple stripes on his arm would be believable. Armed with the truth it was an easy assignment for me.

Lesson one: When there is a problem, deal with it. And tuck away the always helpful thought that it's worlds easier to keep your story straight when you are armed with the truth and free to tell it. ❧

Many entreat the favor of the nobility, and every
man is a friend to one who gives gifts.
Proverbs 19:6

CHAPTER TWELVE

WHEN IN ROME
The ethical conundrum.

The famous admonition to "Do as the Romans do" opens a smarmy nest of ethical questions. Our laws make it pretty clear that customary or not, bribes and kickbacks are not lawful. And while ethical behavior is not about what's lawful, there are times when the two become closely aligned. Gifts that are considered no problem here in North America can be problematical in some other cultures. Just as routine practices in other cultures cross both ethical and legal lines in ours.

In our culture it even makes a difference who you are dealing with. In one instance a government inspector was insulted and became hostile when an individual greeted him at the beginning of his tour with an offer of a cup of coffee and a fresh muffin she had baked. The same offer she regularly made to everyone from utility meter readers to vendors. While we applaud this public servant's adherence to the straight and narrow, a smile and a "no thank you" would have done just as well.

The line between acceptable and unacceptable giving is usually pretty much a common sense call here at home. It's when you travel outside the country that things get fuzzy. Often the locals you hire to help you in these instances draw you into places where you are not comfortable. That's when you have to decide if the business you are pursuing is worth the price. Ask yourself, would you want the deal to be the subject of a radio talk show back home? That should help clear up any fuzziness.

I ran across this piece on the subject by Michael Chan, a young man with a Pacific Rim perspective. I think it's instructive to see some of these issues through the eyes of one who developed his standards in another culture. While I respect his religious viewpoint, I think his core message resonates in any context.

A Gift and a Bribe - The Difference in Biblical Terms

By Michael Chan

Many Westerners who come over to oriental societies have to immediately grapple with one reality - the strong culture and presence of gifts-giving and even bribery that takes place in our societies. It can range from the blatant (Indonesia or Vietnam) to the indirect (China or Philippines) to the "legalised and regulated" (Singapore!).

I remembered my first encounter with gifts as a teacher — I got a very expensive book from a parent. It was very, very difficult for me to return that gift without offending the parent so I approached my principal for advice. Public servants in Singapore (of whom teachers are a part of) have very strict instructions regarding gifts (declare value, report to superiors, etc), to avoid any problems or even appearance of bribery. I decided to make that book publicly available to all my colleagues.

Over at the Shanghai Singapore International School, I encountered Korean parents — and I realized that Korean parents took their gift-giving very seriously. It's something like a mark of respect or even "face" to them to present a gift of nominal value (chocolates, for example) to a teacher they respect. But since I'm no longer a public servant, I could accept them without any problem.

There was one gift I had to return though, and that really destroyed my relationship with the parent (sigh). It was a very beautiful idol of some Indonesian tribe or something, which we suspect to be a totem of some sort. I don't think it's very appropriate for a Christian family to have this in the house so I wrote a card explaining my position and returned the gift. That parent never spoke to me again.

I know that God has very serious instructions regarding bribery.

"And you shall take no bribe, for a bribe blinds the discerning and perverts the words of the righteous." Exodus 23:8

"You shall not pervert justice; you shall not show partiality, nor take a bribe, for a bribe blinds the eyes of the wise and twists the words of the righteous." Deuteronomy 16:19

"A wicked man accepts a bribe behind the back, to pervert the ways of justice." Proverbs 17:23

In other words, bribes are given to blind the eyes and to pervert justice. When money is given for the judge to award you his judgment, that's a bribe. When money is given for a person to award you the contract, even if other parties obviously give the better deal, that's a bribe.

How about gifts? What does the Bible say about gifts (remember that the Hebrew society is an oriental one)?

"Many entreat the favor of the nobility, and every man is a friend to one who gives gifts." Proverbs 19:6

"A man's gift maketh room for him, and bringeth him before great men." Proverbs 18:16

I think it is very clear here — a gift is an introduction, a means to put ourselves in good standing before a person in an oriental society (I suspect it works in western societies as well!). Herein lies the great power of the oft-acclaimed Chinese guanxi, which literally means "connections" or "relations". You can get guanxi by being a childhood friend or relative, or by being friends later in life (mostly through gifts — monetary, in kind or by being the leverage for your own personal guanxi elsewhere).

What gifts have I given so far that ha[ve] given me some of th is guanxi? I've a friend who has connections with government officials — she likes me, and I've been a great help to her in establishing herself in Singapore. I've leveraged upon my network to create opportunities for the school to perform in public venues — both sides are happy in the process.

I learned one thing though — that ultimately, we need to be discerning over what constitutes a bribe and what constitutes a gift (I suspect many of my definitions of "gifts" are considered bribes by most governments of today). I believe that as long as we are sure we are not perverting justice or blinding the eyes of the decision-maker, any gifts we give to make room for us in high places would be regarded by God as wisdom. And what is the value God has placed upon wisdom?

"My son, if you receive my words, And treasure my commands within you, So that you incline your ear to wisdom, And apply your heart to understanding; Yes, if you cry out for discernment, And lift up your voice for understanding, If you seek her as silver, And search for her as for hidden treasures; Then you will understand the fear of the Lord, And find the knowledge of God. For the Lord gives wisdom; From His mouth come knowledge and understanding;"
Proverbs 2:1-6 ❧

Michael Chan used to be a teacher, before he left to run a managed fund. When his business failed, he returned to teaching, and is currently a Department Head at the Shanghai Singapore International School.

He constantly applies his business acumen to his job, to add value to his employer. His thoughts on K-12 education and on financial education can be found in his blog at http://www.senseimichael.com

Reprinted by permission of the author. Article Source: http://EzineArticles.com/?expert=Michael_Chan

Ethics at work is often not the simple
choice of right versus wrong,
but of reconciling competing 'rights'.
Michael Rion

CHAPTER THIRTEEN

IT'S NOT ALL FUN & GAMES
The ethical road is
fraught with curves,
bumps and potholes.

Just as there are those who choose to follow a more devious path in their business life, there are those who see leaders who are trying to do the right thing as patsies, waiting to be taken. Or to be trampled on in an effort to pass them by. Doing the right thing does not imply that you have to fall prostrate to make it more convenient for those who wish to walk all over you. But sometimes we are faced with hard choices.

There's a famous story about the fellow who lived the biblical charge to turn the other cheek. When asked by a troublemaker he confirmed his belief and promptly was slapped. He turned the other cheek and took another blow. He then coldcocked his assailant and quietly said, "There's nothing in the Bible about what to do when you run out of cheeks."

Violence solves nothing, but there's no place in any organization for those who are out of step with the culture. In those cases the right thing is to show them the door, without rancor, without vengeance.

Doing the right thing is sometimes confused with paternalism. They're very different. A paternalistic culture is damaging to any organization and more so to those it aims to protect. When a person holds a job that for whatever reason they cannot fill, they usually know it. Sometimes they find ways to justify their unearned paychecks, but deep in their hearts they know it's wrong and they poison the culture.

Worse off are those who have been shoved aside into a meaningless job by paternalistic managers to avoid terminating them. One such individual was rotting in a barren office that I came across when I moved into a new job many years ago. He was an alcoholic who sat all day behind an empty desk sipping booze and quietly sobbing. I learned that he had been a successful executive with the company before he succumbed to this curse. When he was no longer able to carry on, the well-meaning paternalistic owner, thinking he was doing the right thing, had quietly stripped him of his responsibilities and left him sitting in his office with nothing to do.

In the ensuing fifteen years leading up to the time I came on the scene, his office had been stripped of its furniture and he was left with a beat-up metal desk and a chair. He didn't have a chair for a visitor or even a wastebasket. Other employees either ignored him or treated him with distain. His wife dropped him off every morning and picked him up at day's end. He died not long after I met him. At his wake his wife came up to me and thanked me. She said, "You are the only person who took time to care about Frank [not his real name] in many years. The others forgot he was alive."

Even the worst workplaces in the country have addiction treatment programs these days, but they were not as prevalent at the time Frank was ensnared. The company's choices were limited, but he would likely have been better off if they had fired him with a generous severance package. If he had hit bottom, perhaps he might have been able to help himself. His family did benefit from another fifteen years of a regular paycheck, even though it never was raised a dime from the time he was sidelined. And they received his pension after his death, a benefit they would have gotten in any case. But we can only imagine what they endured living with their husband and father drowning in alcohol all those years.

Not all cases of paternalism are this dramatic or destructive, but they are all harmful to those who find themselves under its protection, harmful to the organization, and harmful to the team members who are pulling their weight.

All leaders make hiring mistakes or have people the organization has outgrown. In those cases the right thing means terminating them in a humane manner. In some cases individuals just aren't doing their job anymore. It is important in these cases to be sure that there are not circumstances that can be worked through to enable these people to become fully contributing members of the team again. It's the right thing to do and after all, it is more cost-effective to keep a well-trained person than to bring someone new into the job.

It helps no one, however, to keep someone on the job when they are not carrying their share of the work. It helps no one to keep someone on the job when they are not happy in their work. In either case the best thing for all is to help them find another, more satisfying job or, failing that, terminate them.

I picked up a life lesson early in my career at a major market broadcast station I was running. It taught me the importance of not avoiding an unpleasant personnel decision. One spring a major client told me his son was about to graduate from journalism school and asked if we might have an opening for him. I told him candidly that the young man would need some seasoning at a smaller station before he could keep pace with our nationally recognized news operation. But I said I would be happy to talk to him and perhaps find him a spot with one of my friends in the business. That pleased the father, and soon the young man came in for a visit and some career advice.

He was very bright and personable. I talked with him for a while and turned him over to our news director, who spent some time with him. We promised to help him find an entry-level position and he left very pleased. His father called and thanked me profusely for my help. The next day the news director and I discussed where the young man might find a place to begin his career. At that point the replacement we hired every summer to cover vacations in the newsroom came up and the news director said he thought that the young man could fit into that job. He said he would enjoy mentoring the young man for the summer.

We brought him in and proposed the summer job. He was elated. I was very cautious and made sure the young man and his father realized that it was a summer job only and that he still needed seasoning at a smaller station to launch his career. While the young man worked very hard, he was way out of his league.

As fall approached, however, we found ourselves short a newsman, and so when summer vacations came to an end, we told him we would keep him on for a few weeks while he looked for a long-term opportunity and we hunted for a permanent replacement. Weeks stretched into months and he failed to hook on with any of the stations where he could have done well. Since we had not found someone to fill the job, we kept him on.

In the meantime, the young man had married his college sweetheart and they were expecting a baby. Complicating matters, he was getting used to the union mandated minimum scale, which was about double what he was likely to earn in a job he was qualified to fill. So when we found the guy we wanted for the permanent slot, I reluctantly told the young man that we would keep him on until we found him another job as we had originally planned.

Predictably, both the young man and his father were unhappy. He quit in a huff. His father never spoke to me again. He continued to be one of our largest advertisers (he knew that we delivered for him), but it all ended up in a very unpleasant situation. I probably should not have brought the young man on board in the first place; he would have been delighted if I had found him a job in a smaller market at the start. I absolutely should have tried harder to find him another job at the end of the summer vacation season. He might not have been happy about it at that point, but it certainly would not have turned into the ugly mess that I created by doing the easy thing instead of the harder thing that was right for everybody.

Strangely, the story has a happy ending. Years later, long after I had moved to another city, I was walking down Park Avenue in New York City when I looked up and headed straight for me, eyeball to eyeball, was the young man. Braced for a less than pleasant encounter, I smiled, and his serious look turned into a broad grin as he held out his hand.

He took my hand in a firm grip and said something to this effect, "After the way I acted, I wasn't sure you would even stop to speak to me. I have been trying to get up the courage to contact you and say how much I appreciated everything you did for me. I knew I was in way over my head in your newsroom and I hated coming to work every day. I even realized that it wasn't the kind of job I wanted to spend the rest of my life doing. I am now in a great marketing job here in New York, and I love it."

Then came the important part. He went on, "If you hadn't done the right thing, I might still be trapped in a job I hated, unable to give up what seemed to be a cushy paycheck. Thank you for setting me free."

Doing the right thing can be hard. Sometimes finding the right thing is even harder. The only thing worse is living with what happens when you try to avoid a tough decision. &

Have you ever asked yourself why one person is honorable and another dishonorable; why one is honest, or another dishonest; why one is moral, one immoral? Most people do not intend to be dishonest, immoral or dishonorable. They allow their characters to erode by a series of rationalizations, lies, and compromises. Then when grave temptation presents itself, they haven't the strength of character to do what they know to be right.

Ezra Taft Benson

CHAPTER FOURTEEN

SITUATIONAL ETHICS
Only fools believe the
rules are carved in stone.

To this point I may have made ethical choices seem pretty clear-cut. Often they are. But frequently it's not easy, and the consequences can be daunting. Whistle blowers and those who object that their employer's policies violate their personal sense of ethics, often find their career comes to a dead end or they are suddenly out on the street.

I was once put in the position of creating a plan to reorganize a radio station I was running in a way that I did not feel was the best for all of what we now call the stakeholders. It would break promises I had made to my people and the community. I worked on it for a couple weeks and when the EVP I reported to came in from corporate, I presented it to him over lunch.

He asked some questions and said that it was an excellent plan. Very creative. He went on to say that he knew that I didn't feel that this was the way to go and that my efforts were especially appreciated under those circumstances. I thanked him and told him that I was able to create the plan because I would not have to carry it out. He looked startled and before he could say anything, I stood up, smiled and said calmly, "You can consider this my resignation. I've already cleaned out my office."

He didn't know a competitor had been pursuing me for six months. I had repeatedly turned down their offers on the basis that I owed it to the people who worked with me and to the community to finish the restructuring I had undertaken. Now that I was free of that moral obligation, I was free to move across town. I was asked why I went through the agony of devising a plan to undo much of what I had worked to build. The answer, of course, was a hope that I could make it as painless as possible.

I offer this example not to lay claim to any high moral ground, but to point out how circumstances can make doing the right thing easy. I am not sure what I would have done had my choices been to bend to the will of the home office bureaucrats or find myself hunting for a job. I would like to think that I would have done the right thing, but you never know until the real choice lies before you.

In the sixties one of the most ethical people I have ever known hired me to understudy and follow him as manager of a great broadcast franchise. Bob Thompson had molded WBEN AM/FM/TV in Buffalo, New York, into one of the nation's broadcast legends. In one instance decades before we met, he had wanted to move in a direction that defied conventional thinking at that time and seemed like a road to disaster. He brought the issue to a head with a one-page memo to the parent company president that included a promise to resign if he could not proceed on the course he suggested.

Bob was more than thirty years my senior and I was delighted to have a chance to work with him. Early on I commented that it must be great to be at his stage of life with a successful career coming to a close, with a wonderful wife and two grown children doing well. He said, "Yes, but I am just glad that I was never put in a position where I felt I had to do something that violated my principles."

We all hope that we are never put in a position where we feel we have no choice but to do something that crosses the line that defines us. In Victor Hugo's classic, *Les Misérables*, Jean Valjean is sentenced to prison for stealing a loaf of bread to feed his sister's starving family. What would you do? None of us can be honest in answering that nightmare question until we are faced with a choice between doing the humane thing and following the law.

During the Great Depression, night court became a form of popular entertainment in New York City. In the 1930s the courtrooms were filled with spectators watching the parade that passed before the judges. The city's mayor, the colorful Fiorello LaGuardia, often used his power as chief executive to take over the bench during one of the night court sessions.

On one occasion a man was brought into court for the very crime that had put Jean Valjean to hard labor for nineteen years. He was charged with stealing a loaf of bread to feed his hungry children. LaGuardia quietly ordered the bailiffs to lock the courtroom doors. He questioned the thief, ordered him to repay the grocer and fined him ten cents. He then fined everyone in the room a dime "for living in a city where a man has to steal a loaf of bread to feed his children." He gave the proceeds to the desperate thief.

The right thing is always not obvious. We are sometimes faced with two bad choices, and sometimes the right thing depends on who is looking at it. Not all ethical dilemmas are as serious as finding bread for a starving child, but we are frequently put in a position where the truth will do more harm than good. A "white lie" is almost universally considered to be OK. Why? Because the right thing sometimes depends on the situation. Those who condemn situational ethics are out of touch with reality.

We all have to use our judgment to decide where to draw the line. My friend Saul Alinsky, the towering civil rights activist and community organizer, was once asked for his definition of truth. He replied, "Well, it isn't necessary to cross the street to tell someone how ugly they are." Indeed. The trick is to know when the lies turn gray or black.

You can't legislate ethics. It isn't about hard and fast rules. That's why codes of ethics are nice to have around but not terribly meaningful. As I pointed out earlier, one of the best-sounding codes of ethics filled a thick binder at Enron. Ethics come from an honest effort to find and do the right thing. It's a day-to-day, situation-to-situation effort. It has to start at the top and radiate to every person in the organization.

What is considered acceptable changes through time. Robert Owen, our hero in chapter 2, was an ethical icon early on in the industrial revolution. His mills were the picture of the perfect place to work. His employees were dramatically better off than their contemporaries. He reduced the workweek from seventy or eighty hours a week to sixty. He refused to hire the little children, but ten-year-olds and up, well, that was OK. Imagine that today.

I once saw an old picture of a group of small children, perhaps five to ten years old, who had been photographed standing on bleachers. They were all dressed in black, their hands and faces grimy. Four burly men in similar condition stood two and two at either end of the bleachers. It almost looked like a class picture from a long ago school. It wasn't, it was a picture taken outside a coal mine a little over a hundred years ago. The children had just finished a twelve-hour shift in the mine.

It was easy to see what was wrong with this picture. Everything! I was horrified. But nobody in the picture saw anything wrong with it. If they had, the picture would never have been taken. If the mine owners or the burly foremen thought there was anything wrong with subjecting little kids to this kind of work, they would never have allowed a photographer near the mine. Instead the men and children were posing as if it were perfectly normal. And it was in that time and place. Actually, it was a school picture, but we are the students. It must teach us to search for the hidden unacceptable practices today.

The danger comes when we feel the situation justifies our accepting something that we know deep down is wrong. In the words of Ezra Benson, it's that "series of rationalizations, lies, and compromises" that lead us astray. When we excuse those whose practices usually are in the right but sometimes go over the ethical line with the "they seem to be trying" excuse. On and off behavior too often indicates that the organization doesn't really believe in the ethical business model. They are just gaming the rest of us. That's when situational ethics gets a bad name.

The companies that are truly focused on providing the best working conditions, fair treatment to their vendors, the most dedicated service to their customers, concern for the environment and their community, will be seen as heroes in history's rear view mirror. Bonus points: they will be the most profitable in today's world. Isn't that the kind of outfit you would like to deal with? Isn't that the kind of outfit you would like to work for? Isn't that the kind of outfit you would like to own or invest in? What's not to like? Play nice, make money. ℘

*Making money doesn't oblige people to
forfeit their honor or their conscience.*
Baron Guy de Rothschild

PART THREE

THE HIGH ROAD
It's where most of us long to be, and
ultimately it's the easiest place to be.

Courageous acts are often spur-of-the-moment reactions. Those who take time to calculate the consequences and decide that their principles are more important than their security, display ethical courage above and beyond, as the saying goes. As my mentor Bob Thompson said, I am just glad that I was never put in a position where I felt I had to do something that violated my principles. I certainly don't hold myself up as one who ever laid everything on the line for a principle. I am just glad I never had to. I admire those who have, and I suspect that they were happier than those who gave up their principles to hang on to a job. I can't condemn those who succumbed to fear, but I feel sorry for them. They will never enjoy the peace of mind that doing the right thing brings.

In this part I want to focus on several contemporary companies that have chosen the high road and enjoyed the rewards, both in satisfaction and on their bottom line. These stories are a lot harder to come by than stories about theft and corruption. Good news does not bubble to the top of the news cycle. Fiction and drama do not grow from the business model that has a happy beginning and a happy ending.

In my experience working with large companies I have found that most are trying to do the right thing. Most individuals will do the right thing, given half a chance. Many will do the right thing even when it costs them a promotion or their job. That's when we need to stand up and cheer. And we need to wonder why their employer isn't smart enough to figure out that they are on the wrong path. When you lose the very people who can make you money, you are either stupid or evil.

We have looked at how an ethical business model resulted in higher profitability in several historic examples. This section contains some current anecdotal examples. I also reference examples where doing the right thing did not work out for a company or an individual. As I continue to point out, an ethical business model is not a guarantee of success; it is, however, a guarantee that you need not regret the choices you make in your business dealings.

What's more as the authors of *Firms of Endearment* have documented, a successful ethically driven business is dramatically more profitable than any alternative. Any course is risky; there are more variables than anyone can foresee when you launch any business model. The point of this book is to encourage those who set sail in these waters to maintain the highest standards. If you succeed, you will succeed big, and succeed or fail, you can walk with your head held high. ☙

Recommend virtue to your children;
it alone can make them happy.
Ludwig van Beethoven

CHAPTER FIFTEEN

THE POSTER CHILD
It's tough to create
an ethical culture;
for some it's tougher.

I had a month from the time I accepted a new position in Buffalo to my last day at the Balaban Stations in St. Louis. Over the half-dozen years in the early sixties that I spent in that great city, I like to think I had grown. I know I made some friendships that molded me and friends who remain to this day. During the last thirty days before I left, I was busy saying goodbye to my personal and business friends.

Don Schnuck, who headed a regional supermarket chain, was a friend and customer. Don was a food marketing pioneer. I had enjoyed helping him develop advertising strategies that broke the mold of the existent conventional wisdom. I also enjoyed shopping his stores; they were bigger, brighter, and more appealing than any I had ever seen.

At our last lunch together I mentioned that I would miss shopping Schnucks. He said, "How close is Buffalo to Rochester?" When I replied, "About ninety miles," he went on, "Too bad. I have a friend in Rochester, Bob Wegman, who is way out in front of everybody in our business. The guys on the West Coast tell everybody they began the movement to 'Super Stores' [25,000 square feet in those days]. Truth is, they all follow Bob Wegman. He's the leader in our business."

I made a point of stopping at a Wegmans Market in Rochester a few months later. It was amazing, certainly unlike anything I had seen. Rather than rows of goods, Wegman had created a marketplace. It was set up like a series of specialty food shops. There were real butchers and other touches conveying the fresh and wholesome foods Wegman offered. He even had a cheese shop with an attractive young woman in Swiss garb. Bob Wegman turned grocery shopping from a chore into an experience.

I made a point of stopping at Wegmans when I was in Rochester just to see what new and different merchandising trend they were launching.

It would be more than a decade before they opened a store in Buffalo. Coincidentally, I had my first professional experience with them about then.

In the mid-seventies I left broadcasting and set up a communications and marketing agency. One of our clients was a marine theme park in Niagara Falls. We were anxious to expand their day-trip market and I was looking for a promotional partner in Rochester. I called a friend in the media there and asked for a contact at Wegmans. He said, "Just call and ask for Bob Wegman." I did and to my surprise he picked up the phone. After I outlined what I had in mind, he said, "That sounds very interesting. Would you be insulted if I asked that you work with my son Danny? He is president of our company and is a lot closer to this kind of thing." He transferred me to Danny, who set up a meeting for the next week.

Summer promotions are created in the midst of winter, and so I found myself lugging a collection of presentation gear, a tape recorder, a slide projector and a briefcase along with several blowup plastic killer whales across the wind-blown parking lot outside the Wegmans headquarters building. Danny Wegman had assembled several of his associates in his office. I presented the plan and to my amazement, instead of the what's-in-it-for-us response that I usually encountered in this kind of situation, everyone in the room was soon engaged in ways to make the promotion bigger, better, and more effective. At the end of the meeting Danny suggested that it would be most productive if I worked with the responsible department people but added, "Don't hesitate to call me if you have a problem." Like his dad, Danny was sensitive to a potential partner as well as to his key players. There's a whole world of difference between a handoff and a brush-off.

I asked if he had kids and left the inflatable killer whales I had brought with me for them. Astonishingly, he got up and picked up a couple of my things and walked me out to my car across that frigid parking lot. That promotion was enormously successful. It was the first of many that I've been involved in with Wegmans over the last quarter-century. In every case the experience has been excellent and their people universally as helpful as they are capable.

One promotion offered tickets to live theater productions in Toronto. It was one of the two most successful up to that time for our client, the Mirvish Theatre organization. Again it was Wegmans' willingness to do what they promised and more that made it work for both Mirvish and Wegmans. In passing, Mirvish is another poster child for the ethical business model. Ed and David Mirvish run their theaters, retail stores and other businesses with a constant eye on doing the right thing.

I offer my anecdotal personal experience simply to validate the broader, more scientific studies documenting Wegmans' ethical business model. I didn't need to go to the top at Wegmans to set up successful promotions with them. Their people have great leeway, the sign of a true bottom-up organization. My only contact with Bob and Danny Wegman was in that first experience many years ago, but since then their people up and down the line have proven more than able to carry on whatever the need. Unfortunately, I never got to meet Bob personally. He died after a long and full life in 2006.

As I travel the country I find that what Don Schnuck told me remains true. Wegmans continues to lead in supermarket innovations. Today their huge stores are a veritable food wonderland. Their bakeries offer a wide range of products from high-end pastries to breads baked onsite in wood-fired brick ovens built by artisans brought over from Europe. Their prepared foods are equivalent to the finest gourmet specialty shops. Each store has professionally trained chefs and a selection of ready-to-eat foods. Everything from a Coffee Bar to a Sub Shoppe, Sushi Bar and Pacific Rim entrees, a Mediterranean Bar and a Pizza Shop. Some stores have large sit-down dining restaurants that seat well over a hundred diners.

They have grown from a single traditional corner store in the early part of the last century to a multi-state regional chain with nearly six dozen stores. Truth be known, they could have hundreds of stores if they wished. Every day brings a mailbag full of requests for them to add a store in some location. Wegmans has resisted wholesale expansion, however. They know that opening stores in rapid succession would make it impossible to maintain the level of service and the culture that makes them Wegmans.

These days each new store added takes long-range planning and literally millions of dollars on top of the cost of building and stocking the store. Most of those dollars go into training the people who make

Wegmans what it is. People who obviously have input into the way the stores are run. Every store is unique; the local managers clearly have latitude to make their stores fit into their neighborhood. It's equally clear that they pay attention to every member of the team. It's bottom-up management at its best.

Their people are beyond helpful. They are a smiling, happy bunch. You see the same people year after year, the turnover obviously low. They are well paid and have generous benefit programs. But Wegmans goes way beyond these unusual but not unknown perks. For the host of entry level youngsters they need there's a unique scholarship program. Teens who begin working at Wegmans before their junior year and maintain good work records and good grades in school receive help with college tuition. Many continue to work in the stores while in college. And some go on to a career with the organization. In the nearly quarter-century since its inception, Wegmans' scholarship program has benefited over 19,000 young people.

Wegmans takes good care of their employees and their customers. There are secure, supervised child-care areas for shoppers and a crew of young "Helping Hands" personnel for those who want help carrying out their groceries and loading them into their cars. You can see it even in their elegant restrooms where they go way beyond the norm. They not only offer the standard amenities, there are fresh flowers and lotions. They have bins filled with disposable diapers and all the other supplies parents with babies and small children need when they are away from home. Even the signage reflects their culture. The usually harsh notice to employees to wash their hands is worded much softer: "Don't forget to wash your hands before you return to work."

As Don Schnuck pointed out to me, other supermarkets go to Rochester and bring back Wegmans' innovative merchandising concepts. But it's the culture and the people they should be emulating. Consider: As of 2007 Wegmans has been near the top of *Fortune's* "100 Best Companies to Work For" list for ten years running. In 2005 they were #1. Most of the companies that make this list are dealing with a high level, skilled workforce. Few have thousands of entry level people, some rounding up grocery carts in the middle of an icy parking lot with snow blowing in their face. Then who else has a CEO who can better understand the challenges of an icy parking lot than one who was considerate enough to help a promotional partner carry his stuff on a wintry day?

Wegmans has been chosen as one of the "Best of the Best" Supply Chain Management Practitioners. They received the Golden Shopping Cart Award for Best Supermarket. *Child* magazine named Wegmans the "Most Family-Friendly Supermarket in America." They made *Business Week* magazine's first-ever list of "Customer Service Champs" in the #5 spot, once again in the company of entities from much less challenging business sectors.

Who wouldn't want to be universally admired and honored inside and outside their industry and communities? Who wouldn't want to be in the financial position Wegmans finds itself? Who wouldn't want to be Wegmans?

Why would anyone choose any other way to run a business?

Is Wegmans the best company in America, maybe the world? Who knows? They are the best large company that I know up close and personal. What's most impressive, they pull it off in a tougher-than-most business sector. Wegmans is a private company, so there is no way to judge the level of their profitability. However, the family pours millions in gifts into the communities they serve.

There has never been any doubt in my mind that the ethical business model is the most satisfying and profitable way to be in business. Should a doubt ever cross my mind, my experience with Wegmans would erase it in a nanosecond. ∞

If you get your passengers to their destinations
when they want to get there,
on time, at the lowest possible fares,
and make sure they have a good time doing it,
people will fly your airline.
Rollin King and Herb Kelleher

Chapter Sixteen

Time Flies When You're Having Fun!
It takes a team effort
to create daily miracles.

"More than 35 years ago, Rollin King and Herb
Kelleher got together and decided to start a different
kind of airline. What began as a small Texas airline
has grown to become one of the largest airlines in America.
Today, Southwest Airlines flies more than 80 million
passengers a year to 62 great cities all across the
country, and we do it more than 3,100 times a day."

I excerpted the preceding paragraph and the quote above it direct from
the Southwest Airlines website along with the title of this chapter. They
are probably the best airline in the world. Along with JetBlue they are
among those chosen to be profiled in *Firms of Endearment.* They are
both great airlines, but while JetBlue is fairly young and still having the
occasional, if rare, stumble (see chapter 19), Southwest has nearly four
decades of doing it right.

They do it on a scale that defies imagination. A scale beyond the ability
of any central entity to control. A scale that is possible only because it
rides on a culture that is embraced from top to bottom throughout the
organization. The gate agent scanning boarding passes is every bit as
concerned as the CEO that their passengers have a good experience.

Southwest has it all, except a First Class section. Not that their flights
are uncomfortable; in fact they have nice leather seats, pillows, and
blankets, all that good stuff. They have, however, chosen to focus on
offering reliable, inexpensive transportation without a lot of frills. Did
I mention fun? When things like weather and all the other beyond-
their-control problems interfere, you want to be on Southwest. Their
people will keep you smiling no matter how grim the situation. Often

they have you roaring with laughter. One of the best standup comedy routines I've ever heard was delivered by a Southwest flight attendant. She was hilarious. Several times a week some member of our family is flying somewhere on Southwest. I don't have to fly as much as I once did, but when I do I look forward to it when it's on Southwest.

Which raises a point. From safety issues to weather issues, and these days terrorism issues, flying is a complicated business. When I was flying a great deal I observed that passengers who were most likely to go ballistic over something were those with little experience flying. They just don't understand how little things completely out of the hands of the airline can cause huge problems. That's just the way it is when you fly. Unfortunately, as that great American Forrest Gump once said, "Shit happens." When it does most airlines deal with it as best they can. Southwest takes it up several notches, as they do with everything, treating even the unreasonable, inexperienced flyer with understanding. And as I said, if fixing it is not an option, at least they'll keep you laughing.

It's more than some company policy or handbook regulation, it is part of their culture. A culture that is overseen by a Culture Committee elected by team members from every level of their operations. That culture is jealously guarded by every member of the team. There is a much more detailed picture of just how Southwest does it in *Firms of Endearment*. Southwest spends a lot of money training their people to do the right thing. And it pays off. When nearly every other airline is in and out of the red or bankruptcy, Southwest consistently makes a profit. Play Nice, Make Money. ౭

Integrity has no need of rules.
Albert Camus

CHAPTER SEVENTEEN

DON'T BE EVIL
Sounds easy enough
and Google makes it
look even easier.

Based on these three words, "Don't Be Evil," the culture at Google is about as nurturing as it gets. At least that is the view from the outside, a viewpoint that I have no reason to doubt. Unlike my Poster Child, Wegmans, I have not one minute of personal contact with Google other than within the "haunted fishbowl," as my good buddy Brock Yates calls the computer screen.

Fact be known, almost everything that I know about Google came from their website and blogs that popped up when I "Googled" the Internet dominant company. I am indebted to Google's search feature for much of my research on this book. My well-known limited attention span does not mesh well with long hours of library research.

Its founders, Sergey Brin and Larry Page, managed to navigate the mine field that destroyed most of the "dot-com" startups. Unlike many of the companies that burned cash like trash in that era, Brin and Page had a workable idea. And they were smart enough not to blow their startup funding.

Now that business is booming, life within the Googleplex, as they call their sprawling campus south of San Francisco, is posh indeed. The perks at Google are fabulous. They reflect the culture of the company. And while some of their stockholders might consider them extravagant, they are another example of why companies built on doing the right thing for everyone do succeed.

The best known Google perk is free food. Not your ordinary company cafeteria food; they have gourmet chefs who serve up the kind of meals every day most of us see only in fine restaurants. Employees also get free healthcare checkups, free carwashes, free oil changes, even free haircuts. There are fitness facilities and trainers. Google even operates its own mass transit system to carry its people to and from work. A fleet of luxurious shuttle buses travels the clogged freeway systems as far as fifty miles from the Googleplex. The shuttles have comfy leather seats, WiFi Internet connections, and external bicycle racks. Oh yes, you can bring your pooch along, but if the bus is full, the dog has to curl up on your lap. I knew there had to be some sort of a catch. And just like everything else at Google, including all the usual mundane benefits offered by many businesses, a ride to and from work is free.

Is it any wonder that Google turned up on top of the *Fortune* "100 Best Places to Work" list in 2007, the first time they were included in the search. And they are included among the 28 companies that made the final cut into *Firms of Endearment*, as well as every other listing of top rank companies that we found.

I'm sure some Google stockholders feel these perks are an outrageous waste of company funds. Just as Robert Owen's London backers felt that his practices were wasteful in the early 1800s (see chapter 2). Imagine, ventilation systems, windows, shortened workweeks, the highest payroll costs, cottages instead of tenements, free education for everyone, young and old, even free flower seeds and prizes for the prettiest gardens. Worst of all, Owen refused to hire children under ten years of age.

Like Robert Owen, the leadership at Google recognizes that creating a better workplace and a better life for your employees will attract the best and most productive workers. Google is in a battle for the most talented people among a workforce that has a lot of choices. The Silicon Valley is home to dozens of companies large and small that compete for some of the most gifted folk in our economy. Google is not the only company offering a free ride to and from work. eBay, a fellow member of the exclusive *Firms of Endearment* Class of 2007, whose headquarters are near the Googleplex, offers members of its team a shuttle service, as does Yahoo.

What is the world coming to? Two hundred years after Robert Owen, it is coming to the same conclusion he did. It is coming to companies like Google and eBay and Southwest and Wegmans and JetBlue and Phelps and Starbucks and all the others who understand that the way you increase your bottom line is to hire the best and the brightest, then do the right thing by them and every person and entity your company touches. Play Nice, Make Money. ❧

Be afraid of the leader who refuses to look in the mirror.
Sigmund Freud

CHAPTER EIGHTEEN

THE REAR VIEW MIRROR
Sometimes you have
to look back to see
where you're headed.

Truly great companies stay that way by constantly reviewing where they are going and where they have been. If you build a great company and ignore the need to change, it will atrophy. It is equally important to review the past to be sure that the changes you made are still working, or even if they were so wise in the first place.

Starbucks is one of the most successful companies on the planet. It is also one of the most devoted to the moral business model. An example of why this company is great came to light as I was writing. Howard Schultz, CEO of Starbucks, sent an email to his top people expressing his concerns about the cumulative effect on the company's culture of a number of well-intended changes they had made over the years. While he didn't intend it to go public, the email showed up on a company blog and soon was all over the Internet and the news.

Here's what he had to say:

From: Howard Schultz
Sent: Wednesday, February 14, 2007 10:39 AM PST
Subject: The Commoditization of the Starbucks Experience

As you prepare for the FY 08 strategic planning process, I want to share some of my thoughts with you.

Over the past ten years, in order to achieve the growth, development, and scale necessary to go from less than 1,000 stores to 13,000 stores and beyond, we have had to make a series of decisions that, in retrospect, have led to the watering down of the Starbucks experience, and, what some might call the commoditization of our brand.

Many of these decisions were probably right at the time, and on their own merit would not have created the dilution of the experience; but in this case, the sum is much greater and, unfortunately, much more damaging than the individual pieces. For example, when we went to automatic espresso machines, we solved a major problem in terms of speed of service and efficiency. At the same time, we overlooked the fact that we would remove much of the romance and theatre that was in play with the use of the La Marzocca machines.

This specific decision became even more damaging when the height of the machines, which are now in thousands of stores, blocked the visual sight line the customer previously had to watch the drink being made, and for the intimate experience with the barista. This, coupled with the need for fresh roasted coffee in every North America city and every international market, moved us toward the decision and the need for flavor locked packaging.

Again, the right decision at the right time, and once again I believe we overlooked the cause and the effect of flavor lock in our stores. We achieved fresh roasted bagged coffee, but at what cost? The loss of aroma -- perhaps the most powerful non-verbal signal we had in our stores; the loss of our people scooping fresh coffee from the bins and grinding it fresh in front of the customer, and once again stripping the store of tradition and our heritage?

Then we moved to store design. Clearly we have had to streamline store design to gain efficiencies of scale and to make sure we had the ROI on sales to investment ratios that would satisfy the financial side of our business.

However, one of the results has been stores that no longer have the soul of the past and reflect a chain of stores vs. the warm feeling of a neighborhood store. Some people even call our stores sterile, cookie cutter, no longer reflecting the passion our partners feel about our coffee.

In fact, I am not sure people today even know we are roasting coffee. You certainly can't get the message from being in our stores. The merchandise, more art than science, is far removed from being the merchant that I believe we can be and certainly at a minimum should support the foundation of our coffee heritage. Some stores don't have coffee grinders, French presses from Bodum, or even coffee filters.

Now that I have provided you with a list of some of the underlying issues that I believe we need to solve, let me say at the outset that we have all been part of these decisions. I take full responsibility myself, but we desperately need to look into the mirror and realize it's time to get back to the core and make the changes necessary to evoke the heritage, the tradition, and the passion that we all have for the true Starbucks experience. While the current state of affairs for the most part is self induced, that has led to competitors of all kinds, small and large coffee companies, fast food operators, and mom and pops, to position themselves in a way that creates awareness, trial and loyalty of people who previously have been Starbucks customers. This must be eradicated.

I have said for 20 years that our success is not an entitlement and now it's proving to be a reality. Let's be smarter about how we are spending our time, money and resources. Let's get back to the core. Push for innovation and do the things necessary to once again differentiate Starbucks from all others. We source and buy the highest quality coffee. We have built the most trusted brand in coffee in the world, and we have an enormous responsibility to both the people who have come before us and the 150,000 partners and their families who are relying on our stewardship.

Finally, I would like to acknowledge all that you do for Starbucks. Without your passion and commitment, we would not be where we are today.

Onward.

The first thing to note is that Schultz takes responsibility for any past misjudgments. He isn't ranting and raving, he isn't assigning blame, he is focused on solving what he perceives as a problem. Schultz is opening a discussion. It's this kind of leadership that makes great companies. When the CEO questions his own judgment and takes possession of mistakes, it assures the team that it's OK to make a mistake. That's the way we learn.

Howard Schultz's email reminds us all that it's important to look in the rear view mirror now and then to make sure we didn't take a wrong turn back down the road. Even though the view is, as he says, "Onward."

৪৩

> *If ethics are present at the top,*
> *that behavior is copied down*
> *through the organization.*
> Robert Noyce

CHAPTER NINETEEN

WALKING THE WALK

Creating the culture isn't easy,
but holding it together when the
wheels are falling off is really tough.

The 2007 Valentine's Day Ice Storm that clobbered the Northeastern United States hit nobody harder than one of the *Firms of Endearment* finalists, JetBlue. A series of miscalculations combined with inexperience ensnared them in a customer service and public relations nightmare. As the saying goes, we learn more from our failures than our successes. These kinds of incidents show what companies are made of and how quickly they learn from them.

A week after the event my OPED appeared in the *Bulldog Reporter's* "Barks & Bites."

JetBlue Has a Johnson & Johnson Moment

February 22, 2007

It was the best of weeks and the worst of weeks for JetBlue. The airline was one of the 28 companies that made the final cut into Firms of Endearment. The long awaited book identifies the very best companies in the country based on a range of standards that we should all be striving for. The book was released on February 9th. Just five days later, the company was mired in a customer service nightmare. Flights at New York's JFK airport were snarled in an ice storm that ended up leaving JetBlue and other airlines gridlocked.

Two factors thrust JetBlue into the forefront of the public relations maelstrom. First, the carrier is a major player at JFK, so it had a lot of flights enmeshed in the situation. The second factor was a bad judgment call. They bet on the weather getting better. That would allow JetBlue's flights to take off, albeit late. The alternative was to unload the passengers at the gate and cancel the flights. They lost the bet. The result: They sent planes full of passengers away from the gates to wait on the tarmac for as much as nine hours.

As the storm settled in, the situation was complicated by the glut of planes on the ground. The freezing rain encased everything. The tractors used to move planes around literally froze to the pavement. Meanwhile, the snack foods aboard the planes were gone, the bathrooms were kaput, and the passengers were hot, physically and emotionally. JetBlue was simply overwhelmed. The domino effect carried on for days. Crews and aircraft were scattered across the system in all the wrong places.

It seemed JetBlue couldn't do anything right. However, the company did one thing exactly right: From the very beginning, it took full responsibility for the mess. The company's founder and CEO, David Neeleman, was out front from day one taking the heat. There was no whining, no legal department dancing.

The New York Times reported five days into the event that, "Neeleman, his voice cracking at times, called himself 'humiliated and mortified.'" With all flights up and running on the sixth day, the JetBlue chairman made the rounds of the media with a plan in place to deal with future catastrophic events.

JetBlue will recover. That's what good companies do when things go wrong. They do the right thing and they recover. Like all good companies, JetBlue's values are rooted at the top and they run throughout the organization. As Neeleman noted on CNN's American Morning, "It's not really what happens to you, it's how you react to it." A quarter of a century ago, Johnson & Johnson (another of the 28 companies that made the final cut into Firms of Endearment) became a public relations icon with its response to the Tylenol tragedy.

My money is on JetBlue to be the next PR poster child for transparent communications in times of crises. Wouldn't it be nice if these common sense responses became commonplace? Nothing stands in the way of that goal but finding the courage to do the right thing no matter how bad things look.

The next week the *Bulldog Reporter's* Brian Pittman interviewed JetBlue's Corporate Communications Director. His interview brings out the depth of commitment to customer service and transparency that this company lives by. Ms. Dervin lays it on the line.

Steady as She Goes:

JetBlue's Dervin Climbs from Crisis Mode to Share Hard-Won Advice February 28, 2007

This week's spotlight: Jenny Dervin, Director of Corporate Communications, JetBlue Airways

How would you react to a company-wide meltdown? Would you keep your cool? Would you or your crisis plan (yes, that dusty tome at the bottom of your filing cabinet) hold up under fire? You're not alone if these thoughts keep you awake at night. We all wonder how we'd perform under such pressure. Most of us, thankfully, never find out.

Yet Jenny Dervin is not one of the untested. Not anymore. Neither is her team. As director of corporate communications for JetBlue Airways, she helped lead her staff through what some in PR are already calling a case-book study in crisis response when the airline experienced unprecedented flight delays brought on by extreme weather the week before last—delays that saw customers grounded onboard for hours, and which culminated in what the company dubbed the "worst operational week in JetBlue's seven year history," punctuated by a last-minute delisting from Business Week's ranking of top 25 customer service firms.

"We are on fire over here—every email and call gets immediate attention," Dervin related in an email exchange with Bulldog Reporter as operations began to stabilize and JetBlue released its customer "Bill of Rights." "We have to buy a case of eye drops for the team! We're doing well—we are now hopefully re-entering normal mode," she wrote.

Here she revisits the pivotal moments of a week she'd likely rather forget, discusses the importance of having a corporate crisis communications plan in place—and offers detailed, hard-won advice for stepping up and delivering when it counts most:

How do you think JetBlue and your team responded overall; what grade would you give yourselves?

I think we held true to our mission as new-age PR people, and that is, to answer every inquiry, whether it came through the hotline or email, immediately. We live in a Web 2.0 world, with deadlines every five minutes. If we aren't staffed with capable professionals and excellent SWAT team assistance, we will lose the news cycle, rendering us unable to assist our company.

I am uncomfortable "grading" our effectiveness. That's really up to the media we served. I can tell you that for the first time ever in my career, and in the lifetime of PR people that I know and respect, media questions today almost exclusively centered around a theme never heard before: When are you guys going to shut up? I took great delight in asking our reporters to please note date, time and place in their diaries—the media were asking US to STOP communicating! You can take what you will from that data point, but I will give you another: Over the course of the last week, nearly every reporter we spoke with ended the call with a sincere "Thank you for being so up-front with information. You answered every question straight-forward." Whoa.

So I'll leave it up to our reporters to grade our performance, but from a personal perspective, I am humbled and honored to work with the people I do. Our CorpComm team is extremely small for a company our size. We do not have an agency-of-record, and we have no intention of hiring an agency. It's not about cost control, it's about our company's leadership.

You don't need a third party telling you what you should do when your leadership is incredibly aligned, and when you can trust their instinct as much as you trust your own. We met our own high expectations, and frankly, we did more individually and collectively than we ever thought was possible. I think the motivation was our love of the company. I know it sounds schmaltzy and fake—but it's true. We love each other and we were willing to follow our leader Todd Burke to hell and back.

What might you do better or differently in the future?

We have been reviewing customer response in blogs, online media comment boards and responses to our direct email campaign, as well as unsolicited advice from several PR agencies that felt the need to smack us when we were down, and as much as it hurt to read some of this input, we learned a few things.

If there is a next time, we will activate our web to emergency/crisis mode, clearing the home page and providing more information up front. We used a web application that makes customers click to a page for information. We normally use this application for garden-variety weather advisories, and in retrospect, we should have kicked into full emergency mode Friday night, when the operation simply fell apart.

Other than that, I really can't point to anything that didn't perform exactly to our crisis plan specifications. We had a full staff answering media inbound calls; we stole people from Marketing and other departments to help us answer inbound calls; we had our leader Todd run our CEO's media schedule; and we had our internal comms manager ensure that the company was kept informed from a single source (our intranet and via email). We experienced brand new wrinkles, such as media camped outside our terminal at JFK for days on end, and we dealt with those contingencies perfectly, in my opinion.

The news media may not agree. We denied access to our "house" at JFK for two-and-a-half days while we handled thousands of customers and more than 2,500 misplaced bags. They were not happy about that, but we opened the terminal up again for live remotes and B-roll filming as quickly as possible, when we could confidently ensure that the news crews wouldn't interfere with the airport operation and flow of customers.

How did you prioritize media calls—how would you describe the resulting coverage?

This event was of such proportion that we decided early on not to prioritize inbound media calls. In order to handle the volume, we "recruited" (aka, "stole") crewmembers from Marketing and other departments to help us in the media room. We had morning briefing sheets for the team, and we used the white boards in the media room to keep a running tally of information reporters were constantly asking for—things like, "How many flights have you cancelled today?" and "What does the operation look like tomorrow?"

For reporters with whom we have established relationships, we reached out several times to see if there was anything they needed from the company. A result of this was the coverage in The New York

Times, which scored several exclusives based on their ability to get customer stories other outlets did not get. We honored the integrity they exhibited in handling these sensitive stories, including a report of a near-riot at JFK on Friday night, by making our CEO available to them early and often. Our openness was rewarded with fair and balanced reporting.

We also issued several press releases that other companies would probably blanch at issuing, but we needed our local media to help us get the word out to our customers that the operational disruption continued, and the policies in place to compensate them for the disruption. Our call center was overwhelmed with inbound calls, while also attempting to call customers, so the more our customers knew before they called really helped the call volume.

Whose idea was the "Bill of Rights"? What was the thinking behind that?

The "Bill of Rights" was entirely and exclusively our Founder and CEO's idea. David Neeleman worked tirelessly the first three days of the event in our System Operations center, gaining expertise in the areas where the company failed its customers and crewmembers. On Sunday night, he called a meeting of the entire leadership team to advise them we would issue a "Customer Bill of Rights" that had real penalties for the company, and real compensation for inconvenienced customers, should a self-inflicted disruption of this kind ever happen again. He also directed the officers to immediately correct five key areas that he found to be lacking, in order to ensure that even if we faced a blizzard the next day, we would be better prepared to serve our customers.

How'd your CEO do? What made him particularly suited for dealing with this crisis?

Wow ... I want to say that I'm speechless when it comes to David Neeleman, but words do NOT fail me. David was tireless in examining the operation, directly from the nerve center of the airline, for the first three days of the event. We also activated him for media on Friday morning, before the real meltdown happened at JFK Friday night. Starting Saturday, he began assigning teams to specific areas of need, including contacting flight crews (pilots and flight attendants) to build a database of those available for reassignment. On Sunday, he directed his leadership team on specific actions needing attention and action immediately, and told us he was going to announce a "Bill of Rights" on Tuesday, so we better get it done, with real penalties to JetBlue and real and meaningful compensation for our customers.

As our leadership team worked the assignments on Monday, we videotaped a message from David to our crewmembers, which aired on our intranet. We also videotaped a customer message introducing key provisions of the "Bill of Rights." The internal message was published immediately, and our customer video was posted on jetblue.com and YouTube that evening, once we had the near-final document.

When was the PR team first approached for counsel on this crisis?

This was a slow-burn crisis. We were well aware of a weather system approaching New York and the Northeast. We published a press release Wednesday, February 14, announcing a waiver policy for anyone booked to travel to or via the Northeast that day. When we learned of the exceedingly long ground delays nine of our flights experienced, we consulted with leadership and published a corporate statement acknowledging and apologizing for the seven-plus hours some of our customers experienced trapped on a plane.

On February 15, we consulted with leadership on a new rebooking policy. We issued two releases that day; the first release expanded the rebooking window to March 20. When CorpComm saw that the operation was not recovering, we consulted again with leadership to expand the rebooking window to May 22. The history of the company's decisions is detailed on our press release site here, so I won't go into tedious detail.

At every step of the way, CorpComm was alongside leadership, taking direction from our leaders and inputting our advice as needed on both the internal and external communications strategy. Our VP, Todd Burke, recommended a pro-active media strategy to our CEO, and David Neeleman made the television and print rounds on Friday, when we thought we would be ahead of the event. Being out in front of cameras and reporters was the right decision, and we unfortunately had to repeat and expand the strategy on Tuesday of this week, when we were assured that we would be back at 100% operations, and that most of the mishandled baggage would be processed within 24 hours.

We activated our media room Friday night/Saturday morning. I know I was on an operations and leadership conference call at 2:00 a.m. Saturday morning, and by 8:00 a.m., our entire team was in place and fielding inbound calls.

We are fortunate that our leadership trusts us immensely, and our advice is heard and incorporated into the overall response plan.

Would you say JetBlue's PR team enjoys a "seat at the table"? If so, what's your advice to others for getting there, as well?

We absolutely have a seat at the table. We consulted our CEO on the proactive media strategies for both Friday morning and Tuesday (full day), and our CEO approved all of our ideas. I believe he set a record for most interviews in a single day on Tuesday. (Live appearances on the "Today Show," "CNN American Morning," "FOX and Friends," CNBC; and taped interviews with network ABC, NBC, NY1 and local CBS. He also appeared on "The Late Show with David Letterman" that evening.) Is that a record? I would really like to know!

So how do you get a seat at the table? Three pieces of advice: First: Pick the right company to work for. Service industry companies should have a high expectation of their CorpComm teams—so that's a good place to start. Second: You better be good at what you do OUTSIDE of a crisis. Build strong relationships with your internal clients, and prove you speak their language and can get their message out. Third: Plan the work and work the plan.

Game theory the worst that can happen to your company's reputation, and practice your response. Talk with your leaders about it, and get a gut feeling on how they would likely respond. Would they want to run and hide? Convince them otherwise BEFORE the crisis hits.

What were the worst parts of the week—and the best parts, if there were any?

Ahhhhhh ...

The worst part of the week was Saturday, when it looked hopeless that we would recover the operation, and that the meltdown the night before might damage our reputation forever. We had scheduled a ~75% operation for Friday, and it completely fell apart. We should have been able to run the operation. We were not immune to the frustration and downright anger our crewmembers and customers felt that day, but we huddled and told each other, "We have a job to do. Let's get it done." Because we did not have data to show that we had control of the situation, we were open and honest with media, telling them exactly what we knew, when we knew it. We also communicated our company's recovery plan, which included the drastic and unprecedented action of completely suspending service to 11 cities in order to help reset the operation.

The best part of the week ... That's a little harder to pinpoint. We all experienced moments of pure love for each other, just for the simple fact that in a moment of true crisis, everyone was eager to get into the deepest darkest corner and work their way out. The funny thing is that no one wanted to leave—it was almost like we felt guilty for needing sleep or a shower.

After all that, what do you love about the practice of PR?

I love that PR makes a difference. Actually, I prefer saying "CorpComm" or Corporate Communications because PR is exclusive to the external audience. CorpComm is responsible for internal as well as external audiences.

What crisis tips and lessons are you now able to share with other PR people?

On the serious side: Have a CorpComm leadership structure that is in tune with each other on a deep and personal level. The last thing you want is to second-guess your decisions if you think the boss won't agree. Ask for more than you think people can give.

When you have a great team around you, everyone wants to pull more than their weight in order to alleviate the workload on their colleagues.

Encourage people to take care of themselves, but don't "send" anyone home. (True pros will go home when they need to, and they'll make sure the work is covered.) Not being part of the experience that you can all share later as a bonding moment is a HUGE mistake. When you're in crisis mode, the world stops.

True professionals will tap into resources they didn't know they had in order to be part of something bigger than themselves. The gratification of knowing you made a real difference is worth more than money or kudos. Be kind to each other. Reward the team with meaningful things—make sure senior leadership knows what they're doing without bragging or martyrdom. No one likes a martyr. The old PR saying applies: No heroes, no martyrs.

Finally, keep a sense of humor. I include in this category the life skill of knowing that the crisis is not happening TO YOU, but you are the solution.

Brian Pittman

No one functions perfectly. JetBlue got a lot of the media attention during this incident, but they were by no means the only airline that left folks waiting on the tarmac for unacceptable time periods. Several others were no better at handling the situation on the ground, and they were a lot less forthcoming with their customers and the media.

JetBlue was in the spotlight because of the number of flights impacted and because they were in the media center of the world. But you never heard that from them. They never made excuses; they focused on telling it like it is and solving the problems.

They never backed away from the problem. They never whined about being unfairly targeted or that other airlines were experiencing the same problems. They focused on solutions, not on how they looked, and they came out looking great. Media interviews in ensuing weeks found their passengers as passionately loyal as ever.

Is it any wonder that JetBlue and Southwest are profitable in an industry where bankruptcy sometimes seems like the norm? Play Nice, Make Money. ❧

Honor isn't about making the right choices.
It's about dealing with the consequences.
Midori Koto

CHAPTER TWENTY

THE BUCK STOPS WHERE?

It's lonely at the top,
but it's not too bad if
all you have to do
is take the rap
when things go wrong.

It should come as no surprise that research confirms one of the few certainties in business. When something goes wrong, the guy at the top most often catches the blame. And rightly so. One wonders, then, why any CEO would want to be anywhere but on the front line when it comes to ethical issues? Why do so many business leaders relegate the oversight of these issues down the executive food chain?

Worse, why would they entrust them to their legal counsel? I'm sure at this point you are fed up with my harping on this point, but lawyers are trained to discern the line between what you can and cannot do under the law of the land. In plain English, lawyers tell you what you can get away with. They are there to keep you out of court and/or protect you if you land in court. That is a valuable role, but far removed from what's important when it comes to the way you are seen by the public.

The reputation that attracts revenue to your business is a vastly different matter. The way those important to your bottom line see your company has nothing to do with whether or not you operate within the letter of the law. They want to deal with folks who operate at a level miles above that.

And it's not just customers. It's the communities where you operate. It's your suppliers. It's your employees. It's potential employees; who wants to work for a smarmy outfit? It's how you treat the environment. It's how the media sees you. It's ultimately about doing the right thing.

Who has their finger on the pulse of all these areas? It had better be your communications people. There's a lot on every leader's mind, but one thing can bring all those things crashing down no matter how well a CEO manages them — an ethical misstep. Whether it's something you do, or the way you handle something that happens to you, all your good work is worthless if you lose your reputation. Communications had better have more than just a "seat" at the proverbial table; they had better be at the CEO's right arm to tug on the chief's sleeve when necessary.

Ultimately, the CEO must protect the reputation of the organization, but you need an expert communications person at your right arm. A seasoned pro who can foresee how your every action will play to the many publics who control your fate. In the last chapter we examined the way JetBlue managed their way through a customer service disaster. Their CEO was a key player, but he had a professional communications team to help him work through the nightmare scenario. I'm sure JetBlue has excellent legal counsel, but whatever their role in dealing with the Valentine's Day disaster, they didn't get in the way of the company doing the right thing.

If anyone doubts the importance of this issue to those who captain the vessels of capitalism, a study reported in the *Bulldog Reporter* in early 2007 should change that view. I'm including the entire report, but there are several points that seem most important.

- ✓ **The executives surveyed believe that reputation makes up 63% of a company's value.**

- ✓ **It found that 60% say the CEO will be held responsible if that asset is damaged.**

- ✓ **Cooking the books showed up as the most damaging at 72%,**

- ✓ **Followed by unethical behavior at 68%,**

- ✓ **Then executive hanky-panky at 64%.**

- ✓ **Of other "Do the right thing" issues, environmental violations and health and safety product recalls both came in at 60%.**

Here's the full report from the *Bulldog Reporter's Daily 'Dog:*

New Study Finds CEOs Receive Nearly 60% of the Blame When Company Reputation Is Damaged

March 2, 2007

Higher corporate-governance standards, citizen journalism, a more cynical public and emerging pressure groups are placing in jeopardy a company's most valuable and differentiating asset—its reputation, which contributes a sizeable 63% to market value. Global business executives assign nearly 60% of the blame to CEOs when companies lose reputation after a crisis strikes, according to a new Safeguarding Reputation survey by global PR firm Weber Shandwick with KRC Research.

The survey identified the key triggers of reputation failure that if caught early could reduce the chances and extent of CEO blame. A majority of executives surveyed cite major triggers of reputation failure as financial irregularity (72%), unethical behavior (68%) and executive misconduct (64%). Other frequently mentioned strikes against reputation revealed by the survey are security breaches (62%), environmental violations (60%), and health and safety product recalls (60%).

Despite widespread media coverage, and in some cases severe consequences for any wrongdoing, key triggers continue unabated— alleged stock-option backdating, corrupt governance, consumer information security, pipeline leaks and salmonella or E. coli scares, among others.

"Interestingly, many of the reasons causing companies to suffer reputation loss are self-inflicted. Financial irregularities, unethical behavior and executive misconduct are all issues that could be prevented if companies had better controls in place," said Weber Shandwick's chief reputation strategist Dr. Leslie Gaines-Ross. "As more reputations deteriorate worldwide, companies need better reputation radar systems to identify and track approaching reputation threats—33% of the Global Fortune 500 experienced reputation deterioration in their 'most admired' status in 2005."

The following are among the survey's insightful findings:

- *The major triggers of reputation failure include financial irregularity (72%), unethical behavior (68%) and executive misconduct (64%).*
- *Other frequently mentioned strikes against reputation include security breaches (62%), environmental violations (60%), and health and safety product recalls (60%).*
- *Global business executives underestimate the severity of a number of significant reputation threats. Approximately one-third of survey respondents place CEO compensation, online attacks or rumors and top executive departures low on the list of triggers that tarnish reputation.*
- *Triggers that are positioned for escalation in the years ahead include executive misconduct, security breaches, environmental violations, product recalls and regulatory non-compliance.*
- *Executives in North America, Europe and Asia agree that financial wrongdoing and unethical behavior are the most significant threats to reputation but differ on the severity of other triggers.*

The survey was conducted by Weber Shandwick in partnership with KRC Research among 950 global business executives in 11 countries spanning North America, Europe and Asia. Brazil was the only Latin American country participating in the survey. All interviews were conducted by telephone between July 20 and August 8, 2006.

ಬ

Set your expectations high;
find men and women whose
integrity and values you respect;
get their agreement on a course of action;
and give them your ultimate trust.
John Fellows Akers

Chapter Twenty-One

Pyramids Are Tombs
The battle is won by
those on the front line.

A great deal of thought has been focused on how ever-widening communications and technology will change how our economy functions. We have known for decades that decentralized corporate structures with authority delegated to hose closest to the customer outperform traditional hierarchical models. Now we have the technical tools to take this to a new level. In his book *Pyramids Are Tombs,* Joe Phelps, CEO of The Phelps Group, lays out his experience in creating a highly successful marketing communications agency following this paradigm. This remarkable book details a remarkable business model that takes the ethical business model up a giant step and offers insight into the evolving structure of corporate America.

Originally I had planned to include this chapter in part four, with the reviews of other books that add to the growing evidence that an ethical business model is superior to the alternatives in every conceivable way. However, the fact is there is no one who has made this model work any better than Joe Phelps. The Phelps Group belongs with the Poster Children and could even be considered an overachiever. Phelps has pushed the envelope of this concept far beyond anything I have seen or imagined. It is beyond brilliant.

I felt I had a real handle on empowering a team to take responsibility and self-direct their workflow. In *Pyramids Are Tombs,* Joe Phelps describes concepts that make what I was doing look like kindergarten. He has structured his company into self-directed, self-motivated teams, demolishing the traditional departmental organizational chart. In a recent visit to his shop, I got to see first hand how it works.

What does this have to do with an ethical business model? In creating this model, Phelps has removed most of the pressure points that allow self-interest and self-preservation to crowd out what's best for all the stakeholders, especially the customer. When team members don't have to worry about covering their butts, they are free to do the right thing, free to do great things.

While Phelps's model is designed for service companies such as his marketing communications agency, he points out that it will work for similar entities such as law and accounting firms. I feel the basic premise implicit in his title is valid across the economic spectrum. Success in the twenty-first century will be in direct proportion to how well companies evolve out of the hierarchical industrial revolution model.

When it comes to the subject of ethics, The Phelps Group has it written into the DNA of the company. They say: "We are here at The Phelps Group to do great work for deserving clients, in a healthy working environment, to realize our clients' goals and our potential."

How does The Phelps Group define a "deserving" client?
- Those whose products or services enrich lives and contribute to a better world.
- Those who enjoy mutually rewarding relationships with our associates.
- Those who treat team members and business partners in an ethical manner.
- Those who provide us with honest, timely feedback.
- Those who value our services as an important part of their success.
- Those who strive to allow reasonable time for jobs to be produced in a quality manner.
- Those who allow us to make a reasonable profit on the services we provide.[7]

Sounds a lot like the criteria the authors of *Firms of Endearment* used to select those profiled in their book. Anyone who wants to succeed in today's fast changing business climate will benefit from reading Joe Phelps's *Pyramids Are Tombs*. And from the underlying concept that moves decision making closest to the customer.

---

[7] Portions of this chapter are excerpted from *Pyramids Are Tombs*, Joe Phelps, IMC Publishing. Copyright 2002 with permission of the author.

This is the same concept Peter Drucker advanced in the 1930s. The one General Motors and other North American companies rejected. The one Japanese companies adopted to rebuild their postwar economy. The one Toyota has followed to the head of the class. The one that weighs the words of those who sweep the floors along with those of the CEO.

Shortly after my visit to The Phelps Group, the public relations journal, *Bulldog Reporter*, published an interview with Joe Phelps. Editor Brian Pittman did a great job plumbing Phelps's thinking:

Pyramids Are Tombs
Agency Exec, Author Joe Phelps Flattens Corporate Culture

April 24, 2007 This week's profile: Joe Phelps, CEO, The Phelps Group

There's a better way to organize your business than the traditional, hierarchical approach, believes marketing and communications veteran Joe Phelps—who advocates empowered, self-directed teams over command-and-control management models.

Phelps practices what he preaches. For starters, his eponymous Santa Monica agency has been featured in business publications from Inc. to the trades—due in no small part to its unorthodox organizational structure and creative work environment, which attracts top talent and clients alike. What's more, Phelps' revolutionary business model is used as a case study at several universities, including Northwestern, Colorado, Pepperdine and USC.

The good news: Phelps isn't afraid to share the secret of The Phelps Group's success. In fact, his management book Pyramids Are Tombs *commits 300+ pages to outlining exactly how others can apply the same groundbreaking principles to grow their businesses and enjoy greater productivity, retention and returns. This interview is a primer for anybody seeking new ways of working... and fair warning to the rest:*

What is the #1 thing wrong with the agency world today and how agencies are being managed?

There's not enough trust from top management in the people who actually do the work. Companies are using top-down, command-and-control structures—which hinders the processes, which hinders the performances. People respond positively to trust. It's a form of love. The more you trust them, the more they trust you, and it becomes an upward spiral.

How does that apply to the concept that "pyramids are tombs"?

The siloed, pyramid-type structures are a death-knell to people's productivity. The typical organization's design has so much inherent conflict of interest that people waste precious time talking internal politics, fighting budget turf wars and such.

What's wrong with top-down management—why the impetus for change (and why now)?

That's a great question. I wrote a 300-page book about that! Now, let's see if I can give you a reasonably short answer.

Companies and their customers want things faster, better and for less than they paid before. And if you don't give it to them, someone else will. Technology is helping to shorten the cycles. And the whole thing is like a cyclotron that continues to accelerate and create pressure on the current systems. Where does it stop? Who knows? But here's an analogy: A racecar driver is used to being in races that average 120 miles an hour. One day he shows up at the track and finds that the average speed is 200 mph. He's not going to make incremental changes to his car and be able to compete. He needs a different car. It's the same challenge businesses are facing today.

Incremental change won't cut it. These hierarchical structures worked fine for factories and the military for a long time. But so much has changed. People's work is knowledge based now. So if you believe you're being paid to think, then your organization should reflect that. Also, we no longer have the time to go up and down through the layers for approvals.

Plus, it's also a seller's market. There's more demand for talent than there is supply. If people don't get the respect and freedom that they need from their employer—they can leave and work somewhere else. Monster.com and Craig's List make it a transparent market.

Each generation gets smarter. And that, too, is accelerating at an increasing rate. The difference in the lifestyles of the last two generations is staggering. Dads are more like moms. Moms are more like dads. People are solving their companies' problems while they're in the shower and while they're driving. Companies can't have that— and then tell someone exactly when to be at work and how long to stay, for example.

There needs to be more trust. And this trust can manifest itself in a decentralized organization where people are given more flexibility and accountability to live and die by their own decisions—and those decisions of the smaller, cross-functional teams they're playing on.

What are some ways to flatten the organization—what steps must readers take to reverse top-down management?

Here are some changes that will create an organizational model for delivering faster, better, cheaper and integrated services—while giving people the type of life they want to live: First of all, you have to dismantle the task-based departments. In marketing communications companies, that would mean eliminating the account management department, the media department, the research department, the media relations department and so on. Then you re-organize these specialists in teams around the client—based on the client's needs.

Now that we have no departments, we don't need department directors or managers. So this moves the accountability for the client work from department heads to these client-based teams.

The specialists still need education, inspiration and guidance. So move the department heads to coaching positions. In professional services—whether it is a law firm, architectural, accounting, or whatever, the professional has to continue practicing the profession. Otherwise, their peers lose respect for them and think of them as "management" and not fellow professionals. So these coaches need to be "playing" coaches, meaning they play on one or more teams and coach the specialists in their discipline on other teams.

Then you hold coaches responsible for the recruitment, inspiration and education of the specialists in their disciplines. Coaches recruit, consult, guide, inspire and encourage these specialists, but do not take on the final responsibility for the specialists' work. This accountability must remain with the individuals and within the client-based teams. Otherwise, you'd be back to those damned departments again.

Then, the question becomes, "How do you keep it from being just a bunch of small, independent teams operating under one roof? And how do you draw on the brainpower of the larger organization?"

Our answer at The Phelps Group has been that we've invented various mechanisms to give individuals and teams liberal amounts of constructive feedback on their work and interpersonal performance. People want to give and receive feedback. But the deadline pressures of their own work often get in the way of their asking or giving. So we interrupt our associates' days with things like the BrainBangers' Ball, the Eyeball, the Playground, the eBanger and even the WallBanger. They're fun. They usually involve food.

They're educational. They prevent myopia, confirm good work, expose poor work—and what's almost unbelievable is that the entire company (there are about 65 of us) sees virtually every significant project coming through the agency and has multiple opportunities to offer feedback or collaborate with the team that's responsible for the work.

In the departmentalized world, you might have task-based departments competing for the clients' budgets. Think of how the multi-national agencies have purchased interactive companies, PR firms, advertising agencies and so forth. And now think of how they compete for the clients' budgets because their own salaries depend on how much revenue they can pull through their departments. By eliminating those silos and organizing around the clients' needs, you've eliminated conflicts of interest and aligned a team of specialists to work for the benefit of the client.

This is the "Mother Lode" of what we're talking about.

One more thing that's important: Buckminster Fuller said something like, "First we create our environment, then it creates us." So the physical set up means a lot. You can't claim to have a flat organization and then stratify people by the size and location of their workspaces. You have to walk the talk. At The Phelps Group, we all change workstations every year. I've been in nine different locations. There are all sorts of advantages to this, and the main one is that it promotes an understanding that physical location and size of workstation do not relate to seniority or power.

What exactly does a self-directed team look like in a PR agency?

A team made up with someone from every discipline in the house moves through a situation analysis, comes to conclusions and works with the client to establish objectives. They then develop various strategies for success. Then, based on that strategy, you staff the client-based team with whatever specialists are needed—a researcher, writer, media relations, public affairs specialists, events producer and whoever else is needed to execute the plan.

Creativity or staff—which is an agency's greatest asset?

Let me think about that one. Well, if you mean by "creativity" the ability to get the job done, then I'd say creativity. I suppose an agency could be a few people using freelancers—kind of virtual. But those people really are the staff. They're just more transient.

How can readers boost their team's creativity?

There are lots of books written about this subject. Jack Foster has a great one out called How to Get Ideas. *Jack studied the processes for some of the great creators over the past 1000 years or so. One common thread was that they fed their brains with a challenge and then allowed an incubation period for their sub-conscious to work on it. Then shazam! So that incubation time is important.*

However, with the time compression that we're experiencing nowadays, that incubation time is rare. And since you can't force people to have great ideas in a short period of time, the way we do it at The Phelps Group is simply to put more brains on the business. Our BrainBanger's Ball, our Wall and other feedback mechanisms focus the brains of the entire organization on a client's challenge—while leaving the authority and responsibility with the client-based team.

This can only happen if a company has an environment and culture that has low levels of fear. Otherwise, people are going to be afraid to criticize others' work. They're going to be afraid to offer a whacky idea. They're going to feel the need to be defensive about their own ideas, instead of listening to criticism.

There's a new book out now, What Happy Companies Know. *Its premise is that happier people are more productive. And to increase productivity of great ideas, you need to keep people working and living from their neo-cortex portion of their brain. An environment of fear keeps them operating from their reptilian and/or mammalian brain—some call it the old brain.*

And that's not where creativity is spawned. About all you know how to do when operating from those portions of your nervous system is to freeze, fight or flee—not a good place to be operating from when trying to create break-though ideas. By the way, I think the authors of that book mention The Phelps Group and IDEO more than any other companies as examples of how to operate a company so people can be at their best.

Why is job satisfaction so important in the PR business—is there a lot of turnover on the agency side compared to corporate side?

I don't know what the numbers are on the client side—those averages differ by industry. On the agency side, though, I've heard the average is around 2.5 years now. Our agency's average tenure is 6.4 years. And that's with 20% of our people being new to the agency for less than six months because of a web-related growth spurt we've been experiencing.

And I do believe that happier people are more productive. Plus, I'd just rather spend my life around happy people. Life's just too short not to live it in a healthy environment.

How can a manager boost retention and increase job satisfaction? What must we provide?
- *First, recognition for a job well done is key. Mark Twain said he could live for two months on a good compliment. It's widely known that recognition is the number one motivator of people.*
- *Then, as I said, a healthy environment—with clean, well-lit space; the proper equipment; inhabited by people who care and who communicate in an honest fashion.*
- *Also, people want meaningful work. We're trading our time in life for money—but more important, we want to help achieve something worthwhile. So, reminding your team that everything they do touches other people adds meaning to their lives and work.*

- *People want responsibility—they need to believe that they are responsible for their own actions, and that they are trusted. Self-directed teams give people clear responsibility.*
- *People need to be and want to be held accountable. There's a feeling of ownership and of outcomes. It's a sense of the proverbial buck stopping with every single person and not in the lap of someone far down the line. People on self-directed teams willingly hold each other accountable, as well as themselves. Accountability helps people follow through with their commitments.*
- *The compensation must be equitable, and linked not to longevity or rank, but to performance. Also important is being treated like partners, which includes a fair salary, part of the profits and some equity in the business. There are numerous ways to do this, such as an ESOP.*
- *Smart people want a chance to learn—they want to grow into more significant positions with greater responsibility. A great way for a company to open this door for them is by support in getting advanced degrees or through classes or conferences.*
- *Everyone wants the chance to do great work—not just work that meets minimum standards and expectations, but quality work: A+ work. Ask your team what it takes for them to do their job really well. Then ask if they'll commit to that standard.*
- *People also need to understand the big picture. They want to know how the work relates to the overall goals of the business. Sharing the company goals and getting input from your team on a frequent basis is a great tool for getting buy-in and creating understanding.*
- *And of course we want the chance to work with interesting people whose goals are aligned with ours. I'd suggest you encourage your team members to introduce great people to your company. You never know when you'll meet someone who is a great fit.*

What is something most people don't know about you?

I was a manager and booking agent for rock bands for about five years. I'd put bands on the road. Sometimes I'd get a bank loan to buy equipment, help them find the right musicians and find the right places for them to play.

And how does that relate to your work now?

Good question. And the answer is one that I didn't think of until a few years ago. I still put small teams together.

I help client-based teams of writers, art directors, media relations, media buyers—with team leaders and team managers—just like the bands. I help them find places to play—meaning clients to work for. The big difference is that instead of taking my 15% right off the top like I did with the musicians, now I have to wait to see if there's anything left on the bottom line after salaries and the lease!

Brian Pittman
Reprinted with permission of the *Bulldog Reporter's Daily Dog.* Copyright 2007 by Infocom Group.

౸

> *Too often great decisions are originated and*
> *given form in bodies made up wholly of men,*
> *or so completely dominated by them that*
> *whatever of special value women offer*
> *is shunted aside without expression.*
> Eleanor Roosevelt

Chapter Twenty-Two

Of Special Value
Miss out on the women
and you'll miss the boat.

It comes as a surprise to me that there are not more women among those leading the 30 companies chosen by the authors of *Firms of Endearment*. Two stand out. Colleen Barrett, who leads the collection of high-spirited and often hilarious folk who make Southwest one of the best companies and certainly the best airline in the world. And Meg Whitman, who Pierre Omidyar wisely hired to take his cool idea to the next level. Meg has grown eBay into an economic masterpiece. It makes one wonder how much more Martha Stewart and Carly Fiorina might have achieved had they chosen a nurturing management style.

Women have played an incredibly important role in my life. Beginning with my mother, whose influence is touched on in earlier chapters, and extending back in our family history and onward in my life. Elizabeth Thompson was pregnant when she was widowed in her twenties with several small children including my paternal grandmother, Alpharetta Thompson McKibben. Dirt poor, the young widow was living in a tiny log cabin when one of her relatives came by and found her preparing to deliver her child unaided. This kind of strength is hard to imagine in our age. Her life has always inspired me.

I remember my maternal grandmother, Ella Forsythe Purvis, as a very old woman as I was growing up. But as I matured and looked back on her life, the strength and determination she displayed throughout her life stand clarion clear. My grandfather, Asa, was a good man, but his poor health threw much of the load onto Ella. Despite their relative poverty, and in an age when most children didn't make it past eighth grade, Asa and Ella insisted that their children finish high school. They all left the farm to gain some higher education as well, most graduating from college.

Mother, her four sisters, and one brother stand as towers of strength in my mind, overcoming a host of challenges that would have defeated most. And doing it all with the integrity and grace that defines the lives of all my heroes. I have scrambled all my life to come close to the mark these forbearers set in their lives. While family anchors my belief that women are central to the idea that doing the right thing leads to a worthwhile life and ultimately a successful life, it is by no means the only example I look to.

A few years ago *American Heritage* published *a* story on the civilizing influence of women. Using the California gold rush as a case study, they were able to document how uncivilized and ruthlessly violent men tend to become when separated from wives, mothers, daughters, and sisters for long periods. The violence and disregard for life displayed in the mining camps was mind-boggling. The article compared violence in that period with other western migrations that included women. They showed dramatically different outcomes. Men simply behave better in the presence of women.

My anecdotal observations of companies where women are major players, especially at the highest levels, show similar results. I suspect that as women increasingly become more and more influential in the top ranks of the corporate world, the companies they help to mold will tend to follow an ethical business model, and it will show up in the good they do and on their bottom lines.

In the 1980s our client Trico Products was faced with competition from windshield wiper systems manufactured in the Pacific Rim and in the Middle East. They had to set up a Maquiladora facility in Mexico. One of the first hires was a young woman whose rare high school education qualified her for an office position. She soon showed strong leadership abilities. When a supervisory position in charge of the most challenging division of the plant opened up, she was given the job.

Of the roughly 1,800 employees in the Matamores facility, 1,600 were women. At this point all the supervisors were men. When offering the most important operational job in the plant to a woman was raised, it was dismissed out of hand by those who had spent their lives working in Mexico. They all agreed that she was qualified, but they were sure that the men in the plant –and even some of the women– would not work for a woman. To his great credit, CEO Dick Wolf replied, "Then they won't work for us at all." She got the job and performed well.

Long ago I became convinced that women could excel in media sales and management. My associate Stan Kaplan, who headed sales at the Balaban Stations, pointed out that a woman who ran a promotional program for us in St. Louis was actually closing most of the deals. We were paying her much less than guys on the sales force who were collecting commissions on the business she brought in. It was a no-brainer to put her on the sales force. She was the first in the city and perhaps in the business.

As the word spread around town, we received a call from the media buyer of a large agency, a major advertiser on our station. The essence of the conversation in much less genteel terms was that she would not be welcome at their shop. An hour later we delivered a letter to the agency exercising our right to cancel all their business on two weeks' notice. Another hour passed and we received a call from the agency president assuring us that anyone we wished to send to his shop would be welcome while apologizing for any "misunderstanding." Irene Runnels became a top sales person for us and went on to become general manager of a major market station. The American Women in Radio and Television (AWRT) established a scholarship program in her name to honor her pioneering efforts.

Though I would like to take credit for having the guts to stand down a major advertiser, at that time our station had three times the audience of our nearest competitor. There was no way any advertising agency could have explained to their clients why we kicked them off the air. It's easy to do the right thing when you hold all the cards.

In fairness to the media buyer, I believed then as I do now that this response was a knee-jerk reaction of one individual to an unexpected change in his world. As we added more women to our sales staff, he accepted them and commented on their superior ability to focus on getting all the details right. Certainly the agency held no such views. In fact, I've found over the years that many of the perceived reasons why women or people of color could not perform certain jobs were pure myth. Today many, if not most, of the top sales people in media are women.

A few years later, when I promoted a bright young woman into a management position that included producing National Football League radio broadcasts, I was unaware that the League had a rule barring women from their press boxes. Opposition at the local and national level collapsed when I refused to back down. Linda Arnold Lieberman took a lot of abuse until the handful of press Neanderthals got used to the idea that she was there to stay. While it wasn't a big part of her job, it was a major breakthrough for women in the heretofore exclusively male world of sports journalism. Linda went on to excel in a series of executive positions in broadcasting.

There are as many women who advanced my career in broadcasting as there are men. I wish I could list them all, but I have to mention two in particular. Marlene King was my right arm for many years and went on to a career heading several major market real estate multiple listing entities. When I arrived at the WBEN stations I found Lois Granite Ringle doing secretarial work. I learned that she had held a couple of tough production jobs at NBC and CBS in New York City, but she had returned to Buffalo to help care for an ailing aunt.

At the time we had a live daily TV show that was a financial goldmine and an operational nightmare. I asked Lois if she thought she could handle the famously difficult host. She responded, "If I can handle Arthur Godfrey, I can handle anybody." The day Lois took over the show, our problems disappeared. She has continued to make problems disappear ever since, many of mine included. She spent the most recent portion of her career as program director of a television station where she created programming strategies that were central in the station's rise to market dominance in revenue and profit.

Unfortunately, many women perceive that they must adopt a take-no-prisoners stance to make it to the top. Just as unfortunately, in too many cases they work for men who force them into that stupid role. So it is encouraging to find women like Meg Whitman and Colleen Barrett heading companies that have chosen the more effective and ultimately more profitable course using an ethical business model. I think it's the wave of the future.

My three daughters and my son's wives, along with a host of women I have worked with over the years, have successfully followed the high road. My eldest daughter, Tracy McKibben LeBlanc, who was my partner in business for many years, stands out in my experience because of our close professional relationship. She is a lot smarter than I am, but it's her wisdom that makes her outstanding. I can't imagine how many times she pulled me back from a really stupid move. Even when she was in her twenties she was wise beyond her years.

Tracy headed up the agency and was largely responsible for growing it from a boutique shop to a mid-sized communications agency with some awesome clients and groundbreaking work. Her nurturing, collaborative management style kept the team together through two decades that she made seem like a long holiday weekend. During one considerable period of time I was the only guy on the staff, and stood in awe watching the teamwork of these women.

Of the many outstanding women I was privileged to work with, Susan Lewis stands out among the most talented. Her commanding presence, verbal skills, and creative mind make her a great team member. Susan and Tracy became friends as pre-teens and she is as near to another daughter as it gets. A brilliant woman, she excels at everything she undertakes.

My faith in women goes beyond my personal experience. A recent *Business Week* story cites research from the Center for Women's Business. They found that "between 1997 and 2004, private, woman-owned businesses grew at three times the rate of all U.S. privately held firms, and woman-owned businesses created jobs at twice the rate of all other firms. Furthermore, women did all of this with less than 1% of the venture capital that's invested in small businesses."

[Business Week.com March 13, 2007]

In an age when a nurturing management style, whether exhibited by a man or a woman, offers a superhighway to profitability, anyone who passes over women for leadership positions is missing the mother lode of this skill set. &

It has become dramatically clear that the foundation
of corporate integrity is personal integrity.
Sam DiPiazza

CHAPTER TWENTY-THREE

INTEGRITY
It is the foundation of the
Ethical Business Model,
but every individual can
choose it for their own life.

There are people doing the right thing everywhere. No company or person does the right thing 100% of the time. Unethical behavior exists in the best of companies, and you can find folks striving to live an ethical life everywhere, including the worst companies. I've seen some of the most ethical behavior and some of the worst in the same organization, sometimes by the same people.

The "Oscar Night Red Carpet Ritual" isn't where one expects to find a lesson in ethical business principles. Imagine my surprise during the run-up to the 2007 Oscars when young actor Ryan Gosling responded to this question from the ABC interviewer: "What's the key piece of career advice that helped you to stand here as an Oscar nominated actor?" Without a moment's hesitation Gosling replied, "My mother always told me, 'If you're making a decision for the money, you're making the wrong decision.'"

Like many on the Red Carpet, Ryan Gosling was accompanied by two very attractive women, in his case his mother and his sister. It all speaks to the solid grounding this young man gained from his Mum (as they would say in his native London, Ontario) and others in his family. One never knows when they will sight a lighthouse of integrity, but I hope the starstruck among the viewers that night noted this one. Ryan Gosling didn't win an Oscar that February evening in Los Angeles, but he and his Mum won my admiration.

In the 1980s one of our clients acted as the claims payment agent for the Medicare program under a federal government contract. The goal was to pay the claims as quickly and accurately as possible at the lowest possible cost. Theoretically an impossible balancing act. Cost relates to the care and time involved in checking the claims to be sure of their accuracy. The closer you look at the claims and the more careful you are in handling the details, the more time it takes, ergo the more it costs to process the claim.

After the program had been up and running for more than a year with ever improving numbers, it achieved the impossible, both the lowest cost per claim and the lowest error rate in the nation. With a billion dollars a year in claims involved, this was a huge landmark. They maintained this position month after month, an ongoing miracle.

The young vice president who headed the Medicare division had instilled an atmosphere of responsibility and a sense of trust among the hundreds of his coworkers who carried out this painstaking work. There was a great spirit evident everywhere, a lighthearted team having a good time doing important, meaningful work.

I visited his operation and congratulated him on the achievement of his team, especially the low error rate, which included such things as one incorrect digit in a claim.   His response revealed the focus that made his leadership so effective. He said, "We are doing pretty well, but given the hundreds of thousands of claims we process, even our low error rate means that we still cause some anxiety for thousands of old folks. We like to treat every claim as if it came from our grandma or grandpa. That makes a difference." Indeed!

I have encountered only a few truly evil individuals. One was EVP of a radio broadcast group that had just purchased a major market radio station in the fifties. He hired me to be sales manager. I was in my mid-twenties; this early in my career it was obviously a big promotion for me. I had moved my family hundreds of miles. When I arrived shortly after the new owners took over, I discovered that I was one of several people the EVP had hired to fill this position. I had a choice: step down to a sales job, or be unemployed.

Over the first couple weeks I watched as he lied to everyone, from the staff to local civic and political leaders. The most shocking thing to me was the fact that all of his lies were designed to gain a short-term goal. He knew as they left his mouth that in a few days, weeks at most, they would be exposed.

He told the on-air staff that their jobs were secure when he knew that a format change would have them out on the street in two or three weeks. Afraid that they might quit before he was ready for them to leave, he hoped to preserve a few paltry dollars of income by keeping these people on the job. He treated everyone in the same ruthless manner. A new manager was transferred in from one of their other stations and the bad guy returned to headquarters a hero. While the CEO put forth a classy university professor image, he was a slime ball, the company rotten to the core.

Meanwhile back at my new job, the new manager and I hit it off well. When I outlined what the headquarters EVP had done, the new manager was not surprised. I asked, "How does he get away with that kind of crap?" My new mentor said, "Never underestimate the power of evil, and don't count on it catching up with those who exhibit it." Fortunately, this kind of behavior is the exception, not the rule. And usually it does catch up to them.

What seemed like the mistake of my life led to a life-changing career move. After three months my new boss quit and took me with him as his right-hand man, and I found myself as part of the management team of what was to become one of the most successful radio group operations in North America.

But things don't always turn out well for the good guys. In another case I watched a simple oversight spiral out of control into a major tragedy. A home office accounting underling found that he had not issued the allocation documents necessary to obtain reimbursement for services performed under a government contract. To cover up his mistake, he sent authorization documents to the division presidents to be signed. They assumed the allocations had been approved by the home office department head, and signed them.

The accounting functionary was not aware there had been a revision in the program and charges for the work were not being allocated as they had been. The division presidents had no way to know that when they signed off on the documentation. The misallocation was discovered within a few weeks by the government auditors. When they went to the individual in the home office who was responsible for the misallocation, he blamed the division presidents.

Amazingly, an overzealous young prosecutor read some kind of deep dark effort to defraud the government into this comedy of errors. It wasn't long, however, until no one was laughing. The cowardly culprit, who could have explained the mix-up, had dug himself into a hole with one lie after another. The corporate counsel, seeing an opportunity to advance if the two division presidents were out of the way, convinced the CEO that they must be guilty.

The young prosecutor, desperate to make a name for himself, offered the division presidents a deal if either of them would implicate the CEO. They knew the whole thing was nonsense and they weren't about to perjure themselves to get out of a baseless charge. What followed was a display of cowardice and incompetence. The attorneys for the two falsely accused division presidents felt that the case against their clients was so weak, they didn't need a vigorous defense. The company CEO refused to support them and would not testify on their behalf. They were convicted of defrauding the federal government, a felony. They were ruined financially and unable to finance an appeal. One served a year in jail, the other was given probation but was still a convicted felon.

Remarkably, no one seemed to pay any attention to the fact that nobody could have possibly benefited from this imaginary "fraud." There was no possibility this misallocation would go unnoticed for more than a few weeks. The two individuals falsely charged and convicted had no way to benefit from it. The company gained nothing. So how could something like this happen?

This tragedy resulted from an atmosphere of mistrust. The CEO was famous for erupting with a violent stream of verbal abuse, often over a minor error. That likely led to the initial error and made it even harder for the culprit to do the right thing. In the end it all comes back to the CEO. The toxic atmosphere he fostered in this organization led to the first mistake. It contributed to the conniving of the General Counsel. The CEO knew the truth. Furthermore, he knew that the two accused men had no power to determine cost allocations. His failure to take the stand and explain the corporate procedures that could have exonerated these innocent men was an act of base cowardice. He seemed to be afraid that he might somehow become entangled in this mess. When he refused to step up, no one else in the organization dared do so.

Before the one young man finished his prison term, the company had imploded. The CEO was out, albeit with a golden parachute. The remnants of the company were absorbed by a competitor, who, it turns out, the General Counsel had been helping in their attempt to pull off a hostile takeover. His conniving was in vain, however, because the people he sold out his company to were not about to hold a viper like him to their breast, someone who might sell them out next. Instead of the cushy position he expected, he was the first one out the door the day the new management took over.

While the two individuals who remain convicted felons paid the biggest price, they are the only ones who can look their children in the eye. They are the only ones who can look themselves in the mirror. The others may be able to justify their actions in some way, but deep in their hearts they know they are forever soiled by this amoral action. In the end, while the rewards for doing the right thing were meager, those who chose the other route carry a rotten taste in their mouths that will remain to the day they die.

Many factors contribute to success. Smarts, hard work, luck (always a factor), and often what I call an ethical business model. My long-time associate Kelly Schultz has enjoyed a bit of all of that. His Mennonite upbringing is doubtless the root of the ethical business model that has served him so well. When he was a teenager Kelly started cruising the streets on trash days looking for any discarded items that he could sell at a local flea market. Within a decade he had established a thriving antique and collectible business. Today he is recognized as one of the most knowledgeable and successful dealers in the nation.

Early on in our relationship another of my associates, Frank Knab, related a story that illustrates one of the cornerstones of Kelly Schultz's success. Frank's father had operated a funeral home. When he decided to retire he started selling off furnishings, among them two very large oriental rugs. After talking to several rug dealers who told him the rugs were only worth a couple hundred dollars, Frank's dad called Schultz. Kelly offered him $1,000 each for the two rugs.

For years Frank's father told his friends to call Kelly Schultz when they had something to sell. He would tell the story of his rugs and say, "Schultz gave me a fair price." This kind of story was repeated again and again over the years by individuals Schultz treated fairly, and his reputation spread throughout the community. And in time throughout the antique and collectible world. Over the years Schultz has earned an enviable level of trust worldwide in his business dealings. There are few people who have more effectively applied the principle, Play Nice, Make Money.

One summer vacation when I was a teenager, I worked on a factory labor gang. At one point I was assigned to cover a vacationing floor sweeper in a unit producing an automotive component. The company used a time study program to determine how many components each worker was expected to produce during an eight-hour shift. The crew had an unpaid half-hour lunch break following the first four hours. I used that time when the floor was empty to sweep up the materials around the workstations so it would be clean when they returned. I then grabbed a bite to eat and sat down to await their return.

After an hour, when no one had shown up, I went looking for them. I found them all in the lunch room. It turns out that they were able to easily turn out the required number of components in three and a half to four hours. So every day they spent half the day or more sitting and waiting for the end of the shift to come. From the company's viewpoint the labor cost of each component was twice what it would have been if the workers had produced at full capacity. Looking at it from the workers' viewpoint, they could have increased their pay dramatically on a piecework program. This lose-lose situation was clearly the result of a rigid hierarchical system.

As it happened I owed my job to the plant manager. I was president of a high school Junior Achievement Company sponsored by the company. Because I was in my teens, a time in our lives when we are endowed with all knowledge, I felt free to spend an hour in his office each week telling him how he could improve his operations. I imagine he was amused by some of my observations, but in retrospect I suspect that he welcomed me week after week because I had added a Management By Walking Around, "MBWA," aspect for him decades before it became a mantra in business circles.

While Wal-Mart shows up as one of *Fortune* magazine's most admired companies when judged by business types, it isn't a universally held view. They seem to be attempting to become more responsive to their stakeholders or to appear to be more responsive. Their environmental initiatives are exemplary. Their push to raise sales of energy efficient light bulbs, for example, is outstanding. While Wal-Mart gets good marks for some things, I would feel better about them if some of their other actions were more in line with the practices that mark ethically driven businesses.

The fact is, much of their effort to improve their image has been focused on adding a host of public relations spin merchants and creating a lobbying arm to influence legislation. Their smarmy effort to look good by surreptitiously underwriting a favorable blog by a motorhome based couple was lame at best. How could they imagine that a scam that transparent would go undetected? Their public relations agency took responsibility for setting up the phony scenario, giving Wal-Mart cover by saying that the company knew nothing about it. What else were they going to say? "The client held a gun to our heads"? Not surprisingly, Wal-Mart has not as of this writing fired the agency. Makes you wonder, doesn't it? If an agency put me in that kind of compromising situation, they would be toast in a blink. On the other hand...well, you know where that leads.

Wal-Mart's business practices don't seem to have changed. Their most recent efforts to reduce labor costs include replacing full-time workers with part-timers who can be flex-scheduled and pulled in for a few hours when the stores get busy. Of course, part-time workers' benefits are much lower, ringing up more savings for the company. Wal-Mart is famous for hardball tactics with its suppliers, a counterproductive practice that has not changed one whit and will prove harmful in the long term. Once a supplier is hooked on the huge volumes they can sell to this retail giant, the squeeze begins. Soon the supplier is selling at or near their cost and if they hit any bump in the road, they begin losing money. With lots of rivals waiting in the wings, Wal-Mart can chew them up and spit them out. But that will grow old, and in the meantime their suppliers have no reason to be loyal or helpful should Wal-Mart hit a bump in the road.

Most telling in my opinion is their "Threat Research and Assessment (or Analysis) Group," an internal security unit. While they contest some of the claims that this unit spies on members of the Wal-Mart Board of Directors and other clearly over-the-line actions, even what they admit is dicey at best. Just the name is chilling. It implies a lack of trust, one of the cornerstones of an ethical business model.

Wal-Mart remains the largest retailer and the largest company in the world, but there are signs that the sun is setting. They are desperately opening an average of a new store every day to keep their numbers going up. Same store sales have plateaued and their stock is no longer the darling of Wall Street. They are hoping that they can find a magic bullet in China or some other far-off land, but their efforts outside North America so far have been disappointing. They sold off their operations in Korea. In the unlikely event that they tried to change their culture and adopt an ethical business model, I'm not sure it would work for them. It doesn't appear to be in their genes.

Helene Mazur, MBA, CFP of Princeton Performance Dynamics, a business coaching company, has an interesting take on balancing values on the road to an ethical business model.

How Values Set You Apart

In business you can't rest on your laurels; there are no guarantees. Ethical standards and staying on one's toes are a basic requirement to sustaining a competitive advantage for large and small companies alike. Facilitating the strategic thinking and planning process every few years is an ideal way to make sure that you continue to pursue forward-thinking strategies. A great way to start the process is by looking at core values.

What do you want to create? What is important? How will your work contribute to others? How do you want to be known?

PRIORITIES
Values represent fundamental beliefs. Values drive individuals and organizations to determine priorities and take action. They influence the activities that people will do carefully, those that they will do hastily, and those they will try to avoid. What are the values you hold so dear that you would hold them regardless of whether or not they are rewarded?

In the landmark coaching book Co-Active Coaching *by Laura Whitworth, Henry Kimsey-House, and Phil Sandahl there is a lot of discussion about the importance of values: "Honoring our values is inherently fulfilling even when it is hard." When values are not being honored, people feel internal tension. "Because human beings are flexible and resilient, it is possible to absorb a tremendous amount of discord and keep going. But there is a very high price to pay — a sense of selling out on oneself—and the result is an unfulfilling life— a life of toleration rather than fulfillment."*

If you suddenly had enough money to retire, what core values would you hold on to?

THE HUMAN FACTOR

While decision makers in business usually focus on systems and structures, the success of any business initiative is a function of the values and beliefs of the people. While practices and systems change all the time, core values tend to be more stable. Values are formed based on past influences and experiences, and evolve gradually.

If there is anxiety between rules and values, the result is often inaction. If, for example, an organization announces that there should be more risk taking to promote innovation, but the people are risk-aversive, then more risk taking is unlikely to occur.

It is almost impossible to "set" organizational values. Values are what each individual really cares about. If we don't really care, no one can force us to demonstrate those values.

Because it doesn't work to try to change people's core values, it is really important to seek out people who are already predisposed to sharing your core values.

BRIDGING THE VALUES GAP

In most businesses there are two sets of values. There are the real values that drive current decision-making. In addition, there are preferred values, which an organization believes should be real, even if they are not. For example, an organization hopes to value diversity, but the behavior in the company suggests otherwise. It is not important what is believed, but what is actually communicated and lived.

Alignment between real and preferred values can and should be incorporated as goals in a strategic plan. These goals can be monitored on a regular basis to see if the preferred values are being practiced.

What values are critical in your business, even if at some point one or more of them became a competitive disadvantage?

THE IMPORTANCE OF VALUES IN TIMES OF CHANGE

A change initiative can be successful if there is trust between employees and management. Trust is only built over time usually within a framework of common values. In "The Dance of Change" author Peter Senge says, "A trust gap arises if management values and aims are not clear and credible." Values are the glue between an organization's culture, people, systems, structures and processes. Values are important points of stability during times of change.

DEFINE YOUR VALUES

While some people (and businesses) can quickly identify the values that drive them, for others their values are so integrated in everything they do, it is hard to articulate what they are. If you are finding it hard to view your situation with objectivity, a business coach can help you identify the values that are important to you, and help you see areas where you or your organization might be compromising values.

As you define a future vision, if you create strategies that build on core values you will be naturally driven to succeed. If you were to start a new business in a new line of work, what core values would you build into the new organization regardless of its activities? [8]

๙

---

[8] Source: http://EzineArticles.com/?expert=Helene_Mazur. Reprinted with permission of the author.

It is truly said that a corporation has no conscience;
but a corporation of ethical men
is a corporation with a conscience.

Henry David Thoreau

PART FOUR

DON'T TAKE MY WORD FOR IT

The evidence is overwhelming,
the Ethical Business Model wins.

While I have long believed the best way to run a business is to consistently try to do the right thing, I recognize that many see that stance as out of touch with reality. When I take the next step and offer my opinion that by and large most business leaders try to run their organizations based on that model, folks are sure I'm nuts. In a broader sense that may be true, but when it comes to this I am convinced that ethical behavior is the rule, not the exception, in business. And that it is more so today than at any time in history. I think most of those who scorn this model do so because they simply don't have the courage to try it, or they are not aware of its benefits.

As I indicated earlier, the image of business, big business in particular, as a bunch of take-no-prisoners buccaneers is largely the result of media reports and what we read in popular fiction and what we see in movie and television dramas. Why is that? Since I have been involved in the media for many years, I have to share the credit for this image. Notice that I didn't say "blame."

The media responds to those it serves. When I received complaints that the radio and television stations I was running focused too much on bad news, I had a standard reply: "We are a mirror of the community. I can tint the mirror rose-colored, but if I make it too rosy, you will no longer see yourselves and we will be out of business."

That was true, but there is much more to it. The fact is, most of us–as readers, listeners, and viewers– aren't interested in "good news." Over the years I have watched as any number of broadcasters –both radio and television– have attempted to fill their newscasts with good news. No matter how they package it, it goes over like a lead balloon. About the best anyone has been able to do is offer attractive anchors and encourage some lighthearted verbal interplay. That generates accusations that the stations are broadcasting "fluff."

Literature and drama on the big and little screens depicting a happy, productive work atmosphere just are not nearly as entertaining as contentious workplaces and nasty bosses. Evil, conniving business leaders make an even better story. It was always thus. Charles Dickens built a career profiling nasty leaders. Yes, Scrooge became a paragon of virtue in Dickens's *Christmas Carol*, but it took supernatural doings or perhaps, as Scrooge suggested, "a piece of bad meat." And occasionally good guys like George Bailey in *It's A Wonderful Life* come out on top, but even in that instance it required divine intervention. We now have solid evidence that it doesn't take the supernatural or any special effort on God's part for the good guys to win. It's in our DNA; we like the good guys.

The problem with all this is that we begin to confuse bad news with reality. For instance, school violence is down, way down any way you measure it. But these days we hear about every incident wherever it occurs. The public is up in arms about school violence. I agree that we should have a zero violence goal in our schools, but let's be aware that things are better than they have ever been. It's hard to keep that perspective when several times a day the news bombards us with everything bad that happens on the planet. And when the Enrons, WorldComs, and Adelphias surface, it's easy to think that's the norm.

In this part I take a look at books and other materials that support my conclusion that the best way to make money is to do the right thing. A part of that is putting the money last. While the capital market in the United States is a wonderful driver of the free enterprise system, those segments that demand ever-increasing quarterly gains are self-defeating. Combine that with those who confuse Wall Street with Las Vegas and some weak corporate leaders veer into very scary territory. Those who focus on short-term goals will lose. Those who focus on running their company on an ethical business model are a lot more likely to come up big on the bottom line in the long term.

The most important book on management published in my lifetime is *Firms of Endearment*. Its authors' research offers conclusive evidence that doing the right thing is far more profitable than any alternative. Books like this make my day. Laura Rittenhouse was way ahead of the curve fifteen years ago with her Rittenhouse Rankings of CEO's letters to their stockholders. Her *Do Business with People You Can Tru$t* gives it all away and lets you develop your own analysis of these key communications vehicles. Joe Phelps's *Pyramids Are Tombs* is another great book, as are Stephen M. R. Covey's exciting *The Speed of Trust,* Linda Kaplan Thaler and Robin Koval's *The Power of Nice,* Judith Rogala and Carol Orsborn's *Trust, Inc., What Happy Companies Know* by Dan Baker, Cathy Greenberg, and Collins Hemingway, and *The Starfish and the Spider* by Ori Brafman and Rod A. Beckstrom.

I will touch on all of them in this section except Joe Phelps's *Pyramids Are Tombs,* which was covered back in part three. Joe not only has a wonderful book, he has a great company that may be one of the most advanced demonstrations of the ethical business model on the planet. He has taken it to a level beyond anything I am aware of, in a business where I have deep roots and experience.

These books herald what I believe is becoming a wave of ethical behavior in business. I believe that we are at the tipping point. Once it becomes clear that an ethical business model is a key to financial success, it will be hard to follow any other path. I believe there are more companies striving to emulate the Southwests and Wegmans. And over the next few years I think we will see far fewer Enrons and Adelphias. While I touch on each of these books in this section, I urge you to put them in your library. Use them to shore up your courage. Use them to help build a satisfying and rewarding business career. ॐ

CHAPTER TWENTY-FOUR

THE GRAIL
Scientific support for the
Ethical Business Model.

Imagine my delight in the fall of 2005 when *Fast Company* magazine hit my desk and I noted a sub-head trumpeting dramatically higher profits for companies that follow an ethical business model. The criteria used to select the companies chosen for the study featured in "The CEO's New Clothes," a piece by *Fast Company* Senior Writer Linda Tischler, included: "How did they treat suppliers, environmentalists, and their communities? [And] How good were their CEOs at inspiring employees?"[9]

All the elements I had grown to believe ought to make up an ethical business model. All the elements I had observed over the years in companies that I emulated. All the elements I had come to believe made for a successful and profitable business. Problem was, I had never before found any scientific basis to indicate that my beliefs were sound. I had relied on my personal experience and anecdotal examples. That simply did not meet the criteria my fact and research oriented background in journalism and broadcasting called out for.

But now at last was a study based on sound research principles. It not only supported my beliefs, it showed a level of financial superiority for the ethical business model far beyond my wildest dreams. I shared my excitement with colleagues and looked forward to their promised book.

What had been a passing interest took a more serious turn when my "Five Rules" (see chapter 6) written for my associate John Manzella's sixth book on trade, *Grasping Globalization,* was published. My "Five Rules" subsequently appeared in the leading public relations journal, *Bulldog Reporter.* That triggered a spate of additional publications of "Five Rules" in other public relations trade papers, websites, and blogs worldwide.

Thus emboldened, knowing that my idealistic business model was not only workable but way more profitable than the alternatives, I began to focus my efforts on promoting ethical business practices. That led me to write several additional OPED pieces in the *Bulldog Reporter* and other publications, and ultimately to this book.

---

[9] *Fast Company* magazine, Copyright by Mansueto Ventures LLC, September 2005.

The publication of *Firms of Endearment* in February of 2007 gave me assurance that the work of its authors was based on sound research principles. Writer David B. Wolfe and academics Rajendra S. Sisodia and Jagdish N. Sheth have created the seminal research foundation to launch a sea change in business practices. They have provided proof positive that the road to profitability begins with an ethical business model.

It is my belief most people —including business leaders—want to do the right thing in every aspect of their lives, including the workplace. It is my experience in most cases that's the way it plays out in the workplace. However, as I pointed out earlier, good news doesn't make headlines. And high-minded businesses do not make great drama for Hollywood producers. Nor is the spotlight ever thrown on them by grandstanding politicians or the media. These facts of life have fostered a perception that the barracuda business model is the norm. I am convinced quite to the contrary that it is the exception, the path of the misguided, the weak, and the stupid.

The work of Wolfe, Sisodia, and Sheth lays a foundation under my long-held devotion to an ethical business model. What makes this study even more compelling is their findings that the companies that made their cut based on ethical criteria, returned eight times more on investment than the average (not the worst—the average) companies in the S&P 500 over a ten-year period ending in 2006. The research underlying *Firms of Endearment* proves that an ethical business model is not only a lot more fun, it is a lot more profitable. What leader would prefer the stress and distrust rampant in the barracuda business model, even if it were as profitable?

*The Good Guys That Made the Cut**

Amazon	Harley-Davidson	Progressive Insurance**
Best Buy**	Honda	REI
BMW	IDEO	Southwest Airlines
CarMax	IKEA	Starbucks
Caterpillar	JetBlue	Timberland
Commerce Bank	Johnson & Johnson	Toyota
Container Store	Jordan's Furniture	Trader Joe's
Costco	LL Bean	UPS
eBay	New Balance	Wegmans
Google	Patagonia	Whole Foods

*30 So Far ** Shown on the FoE Website 4/07 after the book's publication

Firms of Endearment is a must-read for anyone who wants to make more money. Even those who give not a hoot for ethics, although I think it is a tough position to fake. The book provides details of the policies, techniques, and management tools used by the companies that Wolfe, Sisodia, and Sheth have chosen as Firms of Endearment.

The criteria used to choose the companies that make the cut as Firms of Endearment are organized around what the authors call "the five major stakeholders of modern corporations." They use the acronym "SPICE" to define these stakeholders:

Society — Local and broader communities as well as governments and other societal institutions, espccially nongovernmental organizations.

Partners— Upstream, horizontal, and downstream partners such as suppliers and retailers.

Investors— Individual and institutional shareholders, and lenders

Customers— Individual and organizational customers; current, future, and past customers.

Employees— Current, future, and past employees along with their families [10]

The authors make clear that theirs is a continuing project. On their website they urge visitors to nominate candidate companies for them to examine in their ongoing search for FoEs. I encourage you to visit their site www.FirmsOfEndearment.com. While you're there, sign up for their email alerts. There is no better or easier way to reinforce and expand your ethical business model.

Firms of Endearment should be required reading in every executive suite, boardroom, and business school in the world. Those who sit on corporate boards should understand its implications and the benefits of following the business model it defines and supports. It is an excellent tool for directors to fulfill their role in evaluating the performance of the executives they are charged to oversee and assuring the stockholders they represent that the company is following an ethical business model that leads to higher returns on their investment.

Firms of Endearment points the way to benevolent capitalism. It's simply the best business book ever. Best for those in the workforce. Best for business.   Best for managers of any enterprise. Best for communities. Best for the environment. Best for the world economy. Best for mankind.

---

[10] Portions of this chapter are excerpted from *Firms of Endearment*, Wharton School Publishing, © 2007

CHAPTER TWENTY-FIVE

A PIONEER
Transparency Rules!
What do you have to hide?

Open, honest dealings and the ethical business model date to the original honest trader now lost in antiquity. Throughout evolving civilizations there have always been those who based their dealings on trust and integrity. As business entities grew in size and influence with the industrial revolution, varying degrees of ethical business behavior have marked the last couple of centuries.

A bellwether moment for our age arrived when investment banker turned investor relations guru Laura Rittenhouse began analyzing the oft forgotten corner of corporate communications, the CEO Letter in shareholder reports. In the early 1990s she realized these quarterly and annual communications were a window to the stuff companies are really made of. Too often they are pieces of fluff, void of meaningful information.

Rittenhouse says, "The results were clear: credible, informative and engaging letters were more often correlated with companies that had higher stock prices. Conversely, letters that had more fluff and fewer facts were correlated with lower stock prices." In fact, the stocks in the top 25% of her surveys outperformed the bottom-ranked companies in four out of five of the past five years [1997-2001].

This revelation led to the "Rittenhouse Rankings^{SM}," a methodology to help investors judge what the companies they entrusted their savings to are really doing with their money. These criteria allow investors to analyze what CEOs are saying –or not saying– in shareholder letters. Suddenly the heretofore-disposable letter to the shareholders became the smart investor's way to gauge the trustworthiness and value of the company.

A decade later Rittenhouse published *Do Business with People You Can Tru$t*. The book (updated editions published in 2005 and 2007) is an investor's best friend and an invaluable aid for business leaders who want to learn how to provide their shareholders and stakeholders with a realistic look at their company.

Tru$t is a handbook that every corporate executive should have at their side when they are crafting a report to their partners — their shareholders. For a CEO, knowing that your letter gave the shareholders all the good and all the bad news well in advance of your annual meeting makes the difference between going into that meeting with a queasy feeling in your stomach, and looking forward to a meaningful dialogue with your partners.

Her book offers analysis and practical examples from actual CEO letters. Some contain meaningful information and others offer shareholders nothing of value. Rittenhouse points out that sometimes empty CEO letters merely reflect a lack of understanding of their importance by the CEO. Sometimes they are simply overly optimistic, more marketing brochure than a look at the inner workings of the company. Then again, some are just flat-out deliberately misleading.

Warren Buffett is Laura's poster child for straightforward communications between a CEO and his/her investors. The Berkshire Hathaway letters run between 12,000 and 15,000 words, longer than most short stories. As a matter of fact the Buffett letters are stories, complete stories about the how and what and why Berkshire Hathaway did what it did during the preceding report period and what they plan for the future. They are brutally candid, laying out what happened, warts and all. Buffett writes in plain, direct —albeit well-crafted— language without insider phrases or double talk.

All through *Tru$t* she demonstrates the difference between letters that are rich in information and letters that are empty. In one case she shows both sides of the picture by contrasting Buffett's open, informative letters with those issued by Enron scum-brothers Ken Lay and Jeffrey Skilling. As you can imagine, her comparison is more gentle but about as flattering as my characterization. Several other corporate letter writers are included in addition to these main players to help illustrate various important factors in the art of full disclosure and transparency as a way to build trust and loyalty between corporate management and their investors.

Rittenhouse gives the reader the tools to assign points to each of seven subjects used to analyze CEO letters and create a Shareholder Letter Report Card:

1. CEO Voice
2. Accountability
3. Business Strategy
4. Cash and Cash Flow
5. Profit Drivers
6. Jargon-Free, Complete Information
7. CEO Values

In the 2007 edition of *Tru$t*, Rittenhouse says, "I prefer to sum up Berkshire's success in three words: I) understanding, II) ownership, and III) trust. Examples from Buffett's 2006 shareholder letter illustrate why these qualities matter to him and to partner Charlie Munger, Berkshire's vice chairman. She explains:

I. Understanding

In 2002, Warren said he read shareholder letters to determine if a CEO understood his or her business. Our 2006 survey of shareholder letters confirms a persistent trend — fewer and fewer CEOs articulate the important fundamentals of their business success. They ignore five key Berkshire rules:

> ➢ *Articulate principles that determine economic value.*
> ➢ *Understand how to value business dynamics.*
> ➢ *Understand the big picture to make big profits.*
> ➢ *Understand how business opportunities are created – even in the shareholder letter.*
> ➢ *Understand accounting.*

II. Ownership

The Berkshire Hathaway model is centered on a belief that capital is used best when businesses practice "owner-partnership." Buffett promises to treat "owner-partners" the way he would like to be treated if their positions were reversed. A Berkshire shareholder does not just own a piece of paper whose value fluctuates constantly; he or she also joins an investor community where words are respected and one's word is valued. Buffett wants managers who treat investors as partners, not patsies. Ownership has many faces in a Buffett letter.

> ➤ *Own your words.*
> ➤ *Own who you are.*
> ➤ *Own your limits.*
> ➤ *Own your emotions.*
> ➤ *Own ugly questions.*

III. Trust

Buffett and Munger are pessimistic about human nature and optimistic about business. Another paradox? Sure, especially when the partners know that business success depends on people, who are wired to be illogical, unpredictable and self-destructive. If folks can't be trusted, then how can businesses persistently thrive?

Buffett resolves this paradox by seeing people as they are, warts and all. He can read character as fast as he reads a balance sheet. He's not likely to trust managers or invest with business sellers who would waste his time or Berkshire's cash. His 20/20 vision gives him what yoga disciples want: a balanced outlook on business and life.

> ➤ *Trust your failures.*
> ➤ *Trust in doing the right thing.*
> ➤ *Trust consistency.*
> ➤ *Trust integrity when the walk and talk match.*
> ➤ *Trust in clarity and follow the money.*

Rittenhouse fleshes out the sub-points that follow each of these key words in straightforward detail, giving the reader the benefit of the years of research and development that have gone into the Rittenhouse Rankings[SM]. As she puts it, her book offers "the equivalent of an advanced degree in CEO Linguistics."[11] An aspect of education no business leader can afford to be without.

Laura Rittenhouse has her finger on the pulse of corporate America. She understands the strengths and weaknesses of our capital markets as well as anyone on the planet. Her ongoing campaign for openness and honesty in corporate communications is at the very heart of the emerging ethical business model. She has been in the vanguard of this movement for decades, and its growing popularity owes much to her trailblazing efforts.

---

[11] L.J. Rittenhouse, *Do Business with People You Can Trust*, Copyright 2007.

CHAPTER TWENTY-SIX

THE APPLE FALLS NOT FAR FROM THE TREE
Taking "Trust" to
the ultimate level.

The Coveys, father and son, are masters of business. Toward the end of the 1980s, Dr. Stephen R. Covey wrote *The 7 Habits of Highly Effective People*, a best-selling business book. He created a thriving consulting company, the Covey Leadership Center. His son, Stephen M. R. Covey, grew up in the business.

The years passed and in the foreword he wrote for his son's 2006 book *The Speed of Trust*, Dr. Covey says, "Within three years of entrusting Stephen with the role of CEO in my company, Covey Leadership Center, the company's sales nearly doubled and profit went up over 1,200%. During that period, the company branched into 40 different countries and increased in shareholder value from $2.4 million to the $160 million it was worth at the time of the merger he orchestrated with Franklin Quest to form FranklinCovey."

That's every dad's dream come true. As an aging father, I can connect to that feeling. My children have all surpassed me in every way. They have achieved success in their life's work beyond anything I could have hoped for, and that is gratifying. That they have done so within the ethical business model I espouse, makes it near perfect. That they are really nice people adds the final touch. I describe them as "the kind of people I would be honored to have as friends." I'm sure that's the way Dr. Covey feels about his namesake.

I looked forward to reading *The Speed of Trust*. "Trust" is and always has been an important quality in my life. It's the quality I have hoped others would find in me and one I most admire in others. I like this definition from the *American Heritage Dictionary*: "Firm reliance on the integrity, ability, or character of a person."[12]

I differ only in that I want it all. I want integrity, ability, and character. As I have said for years, I expect honesty, but beyond that, I want to be sure that those assigned a task have the ability to carry it out, and that

---

[12] Dictionary.com. *The American Heritage Dictionary of the English Language, Fourth Edition* (Houghton Mifflin Co., 2004). http://dictionary.reference.com/browse/trust [accessed: 15 March, 2007]

they have the character to carry on in the face of daunting obstacles. Miss any one of the three and you will likely miss the mark.

Too frequently over the years I have encountered those who consider trust to be synonymous with honesty. While that's an important part of trust, without competence and the courage of their convictions, honesty has no legs. I have been frustrated too often by those well-meaning folks whose passion leads them to take on a task for which they lack the skill, perseverance, or stomach to accomplish.

I must admit that Stephen M. R. Covey has broadened my view of this attribute. He sees trust as the foundation underpinning all the elements that I espouse as essential to creating an ethical business model. Covey makes a very convincing case in *The Speed of Trust* and this interview with the *Bulldog Reporter's* Brian Pittman:

Straight Talk: PR's True Value Lies in Conveying Trust, Says Covey—Where Do You Stand?

February 7, 2007
This week's spotlight: Stephen M. R. Covey, CEO, CoveyLink

"Trust will make your operations run faster and reduce costs," assures Stephen M. R. Covey, CEO of CoveyLink Worldwide and author of critically acclaimed business title, The Speed of Trust. *"Companies with mutual trust between management and employees not only work better—they also enjoy greater credibility in the public and perform better in the marketplace. This is where internal communications and public relations meet head-on," he explains. "An organization that exhibits trustworthy communications and management internally also earns trust in the public market because its mission and message match."*

On the other hand: "Lack of trust will kill a company's productivity, perception and profits," warns Covey, son of Stephen R. Covey, who penned The 7 Habits of Highly Effective People. *"Look to Enron as an example of what lack of trust in an institution can do to its market value and reputation," he suggests. "The costs of having low trust on the managerial level are high, too. If a CEO or boss has you on a tight leash and has no trust in you—or vice versa—then such a low-trust culture will be manifested in bureaucratic, hierarchical systems and extra layers of oversight that destroy productivity, output and* innovation," cautions Covey. "Instead of the business becoming the best it can be, it becomes a business of people watching people."

Simply put: "Everything takes longer to navigate in this type of environment," Covey says. "Speed plummets and costs rocket. Everything has to be approved, validated and double-checked. Incompetence hides in such systems, and the system becomes your business—not the business itself. At CoveyLink, we call this the 'trust tax' and it's very real. Make no mistake: Trust is an economic driver. If you don't have it, you're going the wrong way."

If you do: "You enjoy 'trust dividends,' where internal trust leads to external trust," says Covey. "It's about credibility. You see that at companies like Nordstrom, eBay and Berkshire Hathaway." So where do you stand? Is your boss or company enjoying "trust dividends"—or are you mired in "trust taxes," as Covey puts it? What's more: Are you practicing credible communications?

Read on to find out—and to discover how Covey's theories can practically (and positively) impact your job, your future and your value, both to your stakeholders and your employees:

What red flags suggest a company operating with low trust?

Companies without internal or external credibility see a lot of spin and manipulation of facts. You experience withholding of information, people clamoring for credit, a lot of covering and disguising mistakes, plenty of pointing of fingers, the blame game popping up in meetings, badmouthing, execs not extending appropriate credit to strong performers, control issues and a lot of "meetings after meetings."

How can a lot of meetings possibly mean lack of trust?

Meetings can be productive, or they can be a means of controlling people and checking up. If you have the formal meeting, and then a following meeting where the real stuff happens—that's a sign that something's not right in the arena of trust. Another sign is seeing a lot of sacred cows that can't be discussed openly in those meetings. Denial that there's a problem is another red flag. Others include: control from the top, turf wars and protectionism, and even interdepartmental rivalry. Overall, if you experience a lot of bureaucracy, internal systems, cumbersome checklists and *processes—then you might have a problem. Excessive redundancy and constant corporate check-ups happen when you don't have trust—so you have to build in backups.*

This lack of trust is also manifested externally. You see it in partnerships that take a long time to form, missed deadlines, quality issues and turnover. Ultimately, it hurts not only your output, but also your reputation, brand and opportunities.

Then what are the signs of a company with trust?

You see a lot of real straight talk—plain-speaking people confronting real issues, versus spin, manipulation and people going through the motions. You see transparency and openness. Agendas and data are open. You can sense if people are sharing their real ideas and data in meetings. What's more, innovation thrives. Mistakes are tolerated and encouraged as a way of learning. That's how we improve. Finally, you see a lot of sharing of credit for success—and little blame being assigned for failures.

Who are America's most trusted companies—and why?

A company like eBay is quite trusted, for many reasons. First, the basic essence of what they do is about trust—millions of people who are strangers online engage in transactions daily. They've built in systems to ensure that. That doesn't happen if you're controlling and not transparent.

Another example is Nordstrom. They are a trusted company with a reputation for superb customer service. That's how they treat their people. The employee handbook is just a business card. On the back it says: "One Rule: Use good judgment in all situations." That's it. It basically says, "We hire winners and coach them and expect you to display that." There's no huge list of policies and procedures or checklists. The mindset is reflected in the company's returns procedure. It's easy. Customers then reciprocate that trust. It happens because management lets go and extends trust to employees. That drives the brand.

Berkshire Hathaway, run by Warren Buffet, is another example. This holding company has 42 separate entities and 192,000 employees—

but a corporate staff of only 17 people! They epitomize the premise of trust. Their number two guy, Charlie Munger, says it's a philosophy of "deserved trust." They assume trust until their people prove otherwise. And people respond accordingly. This lets them get rid of the craziness of checking systems and an overly complex structure. As a result, they move with greater speed and greater returns. That's basically the premise of my book. I outline what it takes to build trust, and prove the rewards.

So what's PR's role in fostering trust, both internally and externally?

In this new global and connected economy, we're seeing peers— people like us— communicating information about companies. These people can be journalists, bloggers or even staff who can become brand ambassadors—or detractors. Trust is the key and word of mouth has become the vehicle. Word of mouth is turbo-charged and accelerated now. That means every staffer is a contributor to the company brand of credibility.

The least trusted people these days are CEOs. The head of a company isn't seen as a credible source because she is seen as having an agenda. That means the most trusted person in the U.S. has become the employee or a peer—a person like you or me. New media is giving these people more voice and power. That changes the dynamic. We're seeing a shift from the CEO to the employee. How do you deal with that? With transparency and by building an environment of trust so you can let them speak for you.

How is that—building trust with employees—part of PR's job?

I think that building trust overall is a big part of PR's job. It's about being seen as credible. How we are perceived starts with communicating our values internally, and then externally. I guess it comes down to this: If you're not deserving of trust, the challenge for PR becomes one of putting lipstick on the pig.

But PR is often seen as a messenger of corporate behavior— not a shaper of it.

PR's role is not just communicating externally. Part of the job is also putting the mirror up internally. You can't PR yourself out of a problem you behaved yourself into. You have to act on your principles. Part of the PR function, then, is to help people at the company become aware of disconnects between who you are internally and what you stand for.

You're talking about "practicing what you preach"—how can PR drive that?

You have to earn a seat at the table to be heard. The first step toward that is making the business and economic case for trust, credibility and reputation so it's not just a PR or communications discussion. We're talking about market share, loyalty, brand—those things impact operations, sales and value. The good news is that most CEOs understand the value of the brand. They've seen the dividends, which include a stable client base, referrals and so on.

So how do you make a business case for the "economics of trust" and PR's role in it?

The simple formula is this: If trust or credibility is lowered, speed will decrease and costs will increase. That's the basic framework for the formula. Apply that to your business model with case studies and present it to management. I've broken the formulas down in greater detail in the book. Start there, then go in and plug your specific numbers in. Also: Stop speaking about trust and credibility as soft virtuals. Instead, show how they're hard-edged economic realities. The bottom line is that PR must take responsibility for driving results and improving reputation, not just engaging in activities, like sending out press releases.

Sounds good in theory—but how, exactly, can PR take responsibility for results?

That's a great question. Start by speaking the language of the business people you work with, instead of the language of PR. This will help you become more credible in the organization. That means you need to understand the financials, sales and so on. Then you need to analyze how your department contributes to these areas. Don't say, "I will communicate what you tell me." Instead, become increasingly credible in the area of showing results on the business side. That will give you more of a voice and eventually lead to your providing input on corporate decisions and behaviors that build trust.

Basically, you want to get in the game. Do that by showing the value of trust, which starts with practicing what you preach internally and externally. PR is the tip of the iceberg—it's what the external world sees. You want that to be matched by the company under the surface. Your message must be a reflection of your actions.

How can a company—or boss, for that matter—rebuild lost trust?

First, you focus on yourself. Start there versus blaming. Focus on your own credibility, character and competence. Ask yourself tough questions like: How is my integrity? How am I perceived? How is my intent perceived? Do I have people's best interests in mind? How do my people view my motives—am I really looking for mutual benefit?

The four cores of credibility are: your integrity, your intent, your capabilities and your results. Those are the elements that make a person or company worthy of trust. Analyze those elements honestly. Then behave in a way—or try to drive corporate behavior—that rights any wrongs or shortcomings in those areas. But remember to do it. You can't just talk your way out of it. Otherwise, it's all just spin—and that's not just something that destroys trust. It's also something that, unfortunately, has become synonymous with PR. Changing that starts with you.

Brian Pittman
Reprinted with permission of the Bulldog Reporter's Daily 'Dog. Copyright 2007 by Infocom Group.

Stephen M. R. Covey and I are singing from the same hymnbook. He has a number of fresh ideas, but in the end it all leads to following an ethical business model. I am particularly encouraged with his take on the role of public relations in corporate America. He reinforces my contention that communications has to be on the front line when it comes to maintaining ethics and defending corporate reputation.

It is important that those responsible for corporate communications look beyond what many see as the role of public relations. As Jenny Dervin, Director of Corporate Communications for JetBlue Airways, points out in chapter nineteen of this book, "I love that PR makes a difference. Actually, I prefer saying Corporate Communications because PR is exclusive to the external audience. CorpComm is responsible for internal as well as external audiences."

The seat at the table that Ms. Dervin has and that Covey advocates for those in Public Relations or Corporate Communications, whatever you call it, is vital to an ethical business model and vital to keeping the company on track. They are the only members of the corporate team exclusively focused on keeping the company on target, "Doing the Right Thing." To enable them to do their job the CEO needs to be sure that a culture of transparency rules and that these watchdogs of the company's reputation have his ear and his trust. Smart leaders keep an eye cocked on communications; it is the canary in their coal mine.

Covey delves much deeper into how trust makes a company a leader in every aspect, including the bottom line. He lists what he calls "The 7 Low-Trust Organizational Taxes." In other words, the seven ways in which lack of trust raises costs and slows corporations down. They are:

1. Redundancy
2. Bureaucracy
3. Politics
4. Disengagement
5. Turnover
6. Churn
7. Fraud

He contrasts those with "The 7 High-Trust Organizational Dividends." The factors that make a company more effective. They are:

1. Increased Value
2. Accelerated Growth
3. Enhanced Innovation
4. Improved Collaboration
5. Stronger Partnering
6. Better Execution
7. Heightened Loyalty[13]

---

[13] Stephen M. R. Covey, *The Speed of Trust* (Free Press, 2006) CoveyLink, LLC.

If you gain nothing else from his book (and there is much, much more), his detailed explanations of how these contrasting conditions of trust affect corporate life would make the book a must-read. For example, under Increased Value he adds to the evidence that companies that embrace an ethical business model are more profitable. He says:

High Trust increases value in two dimensions.

The first dimension is shareholder value—and the data is compelling. As I noted earlier, in a Watson Wyatt 2002 study, high-trust organizations outperformed low-trust organizations in total return to shareholders (stock price plus dividends) by 286%.

Additionally, according to a 2005 study by Russell Investment Group, Fortune *magazine's "100 Best Companies to Work for in America" (in which trust constitutes 60% of the criteria) earned over four times the returns of the broader market over the prior seven years. As* Fortune *declared, "Employees treasure the freedom to do their job as they think best, and great employers trust them."*

Covey goes on to explain how trust adds to customer value. It pretty much adds up to the same aspects of character that I see in the ethical business model. This is a great book and part of the growing support for that model. Why in heaven's name would anyone want anything less than a productive, profitable, and, best of all, a happy workplace? Play Nice, Make Money! ೞ

CHAPTER TWENTY-SEVEN

THE HEADLESS WONDER
Another way to look at it.

Two very bright young guys with a track record of business successes have crafted an engaging book that reworks an age-old rule. As Mel Brooks so wonderfully put it, "It's good to be King." But history shows that while it is often (but not always) good for the individual with the crown, it's not so hot for the country or the people. Their book envisions a business model with no King, no leader of any kind...well, sort of.

The Starfish and the Spider: The Unstoppable Power of Leaderless Organizations plays off the rule of nature that a creature like a spider cannot function if you cut off its head, whereas a starfish, which has no head, can't be killed by whacking it up. In fact, in some starfish species each of the parts grows back into a new starfish.

Authors Ori Brafman and Rod A. Beckstrom cite examples such as the Apache Indians in America's early days and the international terrorist organization al Qaeda, where efforts to attack them by killing their leader (cutting off their head) simply opens the door to another leader.

While these and other examples demonstrate the positive reaction people have to any organization that functions from the bottom up, the authors don't really ever make a case for a leaderless business model. In fact, the examples they use in today's business world are in some cases anything but leaderless. They call those companies hybrids: part spider (centralized), part starfish (decentralized).

In all cases they lean on the bottom-up management style as the sole factor that influences success. They contrast it with what they call the "control and command" style with all that implies in a hierarchical-based organization. They overlook the need for someone to set the tone or the culture of the company. My father's observation that his employer didn't understand "what the men want" spoke to the need for both a bottom-up element and a need for a nurturing culture. But someone has to keep it on track.

Remember Robert Owen in chapter Two? In the late 1700s the young Owen took over Drinkwater's factory with 500 workers in Manchester, England. For six weeks Robert did nothing but walk about the mill and get to know the employees. He was the first to arrive at the mill and the last to leave each day. Then he reorganized the plant along classic "bottom-up" lines that defied the conventional management practices of the day. But Owen was the leader; he set the tone and created the culture, a culture that was a great success. He stumbled later when he bought into the commune culture of the early 1800s, a truly leaderless concept that failed in every case, just as it would today.

Brafman and Beckstrom point to Peter Drucker, who was brought in to study General Motors at the height of its success six decades ago. Drucker concluded that the autonomy its divisions and plants enjoyed was the key to why it did so well. Drucker, however, never suggested anything close to a leaderless option. Actually, when Drucker suggested that GM expand its bottom-up management style, they gave him the boot. The rest of big business in America laughed him out of the country, literally.

Peter Drucker took his crazy notions to Japan. They were struggling to rebuild their economy following World War Two. The Japanese adopted his concepts, along with W. Edwards Deming's quality control concepts (equally unpopular in America), as gospel and the rest is history. Today America's automotive sector is in chaos and Japanese automakers have proven they can beat our pants off by functioning on the Drucker/Deming model. And not just in the Pacific Rim; Japanese-managed plants in North America outperform everyone else, including those guided by the heralded European car makers.

In the early 1980s, Tom Peters and Bob Waterman popularized the Hewlett-Packard mantra, Management By Walking Around (MBWA), in their best-seller, *In Search of Excellence: Lessons from America's Best-Run Companies*. That's what Robert Owen did, that's what Peter Drucker did, that's what smart business leaders have always done. It's the same idea, just a catchy new phrase. My other historic examples and the outstanding companies we cite today all use some variant of a bottom-up management style. But it's only the foundation for the ethical business model I am suggesting.

While decentralized management is crucial to building an ethical business model, the model requires leadership that sets the tone. There has to be devotion to the principles that ultimately bring out the best in every member of the team, the principles that guide the company's dealings with all the stakeholders. That's what I mean by an ethical business culture. It starts at the top. It can't happen without a leader.

With proof that ethical corporate entities can outperform any of the alternatives, this model should sweep the world economy. Imagine a world economy driven by these business principles. It doesn't take much to see that it could lead to more than financial success. It could lead to the kind of world that's only been a dream up to this point.

Brafman and Beckstrom are right on target in their assessment of the importance of any one leader. *The Starfish and the Spider* authors point out that the leaders of the companies they call hybrids can be replaced. While that's true, there's no guarantee the culture will remain. What evolves depends mostly on the next leader; what evolves could become more octopus than starfish.

The mark of a great leader is not what they impose on those they lead, but what they inspire, including the development of leadership at every level within the organization. Most important is the development of successors who can step into the leader's shoes as if they were their own.

Cutting off the head of such an organization has no impact. And the beauty of such an organization is that those kinds of leaders rarely have to be replaced. The wonder after all these years is that any other type still exists. ಬಂ

CHAPTER TWENTY-EIGHT

PLAY NICE, MAKE MORE THAN MONEY!
Books to validate,
books to navigate.

Every day it seems I find a compelling article or book that supports the ethical business model. Books like *The Power of Nice* by advertising innovators Linda Kaplan Thaler and Robin Koval. They have built one of the hottest ad agencies in the country on the principle that "It pays to be nice." Their light and breezy style makes their book fun to read, but it's a whole lot more than that. It is filled with practical advice and engaging stories from their practice.

From the unexpected payoff provided by a warm friendly security guard in their lobby to the plug they got from Donald Trump for their kindness to his wife, the authors document how powerful courtesy and good manners can be. Combined with creative skills that have produced groundbreaking advertising including the "Aflac Duck," these two self-described "Nice Women" have used the power of nice to become leaders in the Madison Avenue marketing game.

The last paragraph in their book sums it up:

> *If you take nothing else away from this book, we hope it's the realization that there is untapped potential in even the smallest good deed, and that it can have a multiplier effect strong enough to change the world. Yes, a random act of kindness can help you become wealthier, healthier, and wiser. But most of all, it will make you happier. And, after all, isn't that the real power of nice?*

If you haven't already found *The Power of Nice*, pick it up, it's a really wonderful read and it will help you understand a crucial element of the quest for an ethical business model.

Another pair of outstanding women, Judith Rogala and Carol Orsborn, have a great book, *Trust, Inc.* They combine some of their experiences as high-level business executives with a wide range of benchmarking and testing to help create and maintain trust among corporate team members. *Trust, Inc.* will give you valuable tools to build and support the ethical business model.

You can't find many more examples of winning ways in the corporate world than those in *What Happy Companies Know: How the New Science of Happiness Can Change Your Company for the Better* by Dan Baker, Cathy Greenberg, and Collins Hemingway. These three successful business coaches, consultants, and authors have jam packed their book with the kind of practical examples that make it easier to understand and apply ethical elements to your business model.

All three of these books, along with the others reviewed in this book, are well worth adding to your library and suggesting to your associates.

ဆ

CHAPTER TWENTY-NINE

BY THE NUMBERS
They all add up to the
Ethical Business Model.

As I have delved into the world of ethically driven businesses, support for this model has been popping up on all sides. It has made it hard for me to choose illustrations to include in this book and even harder to wrap it up. Then the April 2007 issue of *Fast Company* hit my desk with another metric, "HIP, Human Impact + Profit."[14] *Fast Company* teamed up with two San Francisco based firms, the HIP Investor and the SVT Group, to evaluate and rate publicly listed companies. Their goal: to look past good intentions and focus on concrete results –how human impact drives the bottom line– as a guide for investors seeking to generate compelling returns and benefit society. HIP is described as "a new way of looking at the human side of investing."

It is interesting and worthwhile reading. *Fast Company* is consistently filled with thought-provoking articles. The leader in reporting the "New Economy," *Fast Company* has managed to stay out ahead of the latest innovations in business. For this study they contacted 100 companies they saw as leaders. They profiled 21 who were able to describe their strategic vision, performance metrics, financial returns, accountability, and decision-making systems that support sustainable performance. These 21 respondents could also articulate how their management approach drove human impact: namely, the health and wealth of customers and employees, environmental quality, and social equality.

These are the companies in the *Fast Company* HIP study: Advance Micro Devices, Alcoa, Cisco, General Electric, Goldman Sachs, Herman Miller, Hewlett-Packard, Infosys Technologies, Intel, Interface, IBM, Liberty Property Trust, McDonald's, Nike, PG&E, Starbucks, Sun Microsystems, United Technologies, Verizon, Walgreens, and Wal-Mart.

I had difficulty sorting out the methodology used, but it seems that the final scores came from the companies' self-assessments. Even then, the companies studied did not all come out smelling like roses. It's telling that only one of the thirty companies that made the Firms of Endearment cut (Starbucks) is on this list. (Some FoEs are private

---

[14] *Fast Company* Issue 114 (April 2007, copyright 2007 Mansueto Ventures LLC), 84.

and would be excluded for that reason.) A major flaw jumped out as I reviewed the study and the methodology: it was hard to determine if those who talked the talk, walked the walk.

A story by Richard Carufel on the GolinHarris Corporate Citizenship Index in the *Bulldog Reporter* adds to the evidence that business reputation is a major factor when consumers choose where to spend their money. While the index didn't take into account all aspects of an ethical business model, it gives us one more solid piece of research that good guys finish first.

Insightful New Survey Reaffirms That Corporate Reputation Drives Consumer Loyalty—Authenticity Is Key Factor in Shaping Word-of-Mouth Value

Bulldog Reporter Daily 'Dog
December 8, 2006

The results of a recently released survey strongly suggest that consumers are more supportive of corporations that are transparent and authentic in their messaging—and are more willing to do business with those companies that embrace "corporate citizenship." The study reveals respondents recognize progress is being made as a growing number of companies embrace corporate citizenship as a business asset, although business still has a long way to go to meet Americans' rising expectations for good corporate citizenship.

The survey, authored by GolinHarris and conducted by Change, interviewed 5,000 Americans, who rated 152 brands for the GolinHarris Corporate Citizenship Index in September. Results were measured along 12 critical drivers of corporate citizenship, with each brand earning a grade ranging from "excellent" to "poor" based on a single-number index scorecard of 0 to 100. Companies scoring 65 or higher are Excellent performers, 55–65 are Good, 45-54 are Fair/ Average and below 45 are rated Poor performers.

Only one company received an "excellent" score—Ben & Jerry's led all corporations with a score of 68.08. Other high-ranking organizations include Target (64.75), Patagonia (64.65), SC Johnson (64.45), Gerber (62.54) and Southwest Airlines (62.27). Notables include Johnson & Johnson, The Body Shop, UPS and 3M.

According to GolinHarris, Americans are sending a message to business that good corporate citizenship is a "must have," critical to business success in good times and bad. Some items on the survey received at least two-thirds of consumer support. These include:

- *Doing well by doing good is a savvy business strategy. Good corporate citizenship should be approached as an investment, asset and competitive advantage for business that contributes to the company's success. (67%)*
- *Business should invest significantly more money, time, attention and resources in corporate citizenship than it does today. (68%)*
- *Corporate citizenship should be considered an essential, high priority compared to other priorities companies face and manage in running a profitable, competitive and successful business. (68%)*

Moreover, when Americans experience authentic corporate citizenship, they get down to business in their relationships with brands. The survey reveals that good corporate citizenship can impact business results by stimulating Americans to be loyal, passionate and frequent business advocates as well as committed customers to brands that have earned their trust and support. The top ways good corporate citizenship influences their behavior and attitude toward a company are:

- *Recommend the company, its products and services to family, friends, neighbors or co-workers.*
- *Improve my respect for and opinion of the company and its reputation.*
- *Try the company's products and services for the first time if I've never been a customer.*
- *Switch to the company, its products and services from a competitor, if other factors are fairly equal.*
- *Increase my trust in the company and its people, products and services.*
- *Welcome the company into my community if it wants to locate, expand or do business here.*
- *Become more loyal and committed to the company, its products and services.*
- *Increase my buying of the company's products and services if I'm currently a customer, or come back to the company if I'm formerly a customer.*

- *Try new and different products from the company I hadn't considered before.*
- *Admire the company as a leader, influencer or role-model within its industry and as a business.*

The top performers on the 2006 GH Corporate Citizenship Index are as diverse as American business itself in terms of industry, business model, resources, ownership and commitments. But while different in style and substance, their corporate citizenship shares a key essential quality: "authenticity," according to Fred Cook, president and CEO, GolinHarris.

"Authenticity is what distinguishes and differentiates truly great corporate citizens," explained Cook. "Leaders know that corporate citizenship must be an organic outgrowth of the company's business value proposition, brand essence, and everyday practices in the marketplace. To be authentic, corporate citizenship must ring true, be relevant and resonate in all the ways a company conducts its business with stakeholders – be they customers, employees, investors, suppliers, communities or others."

"Americans can tell the real deal and authentic original from companies that go shopping for trendy and stylish issues," Cook concluded.

Richard Carufel
Reprinted with permission of the Bulldog Reporter's Daily 'Dog. Copyright 2006 by Infocom Group.

A landmark 2006 study conducted by Delahaye, a Division of Bacon's Information, in conjunction with the Public Relations Society of America, plumbed the state of that profession.[15] They were able to enlist 1,493 members and non-members of the PRSA to share their views. While most of the study had nothing to do with ethics, a couple of the questions offer insight into how they see their role relating to ethical issues. That this aspect of their work is important comes out clearly in this sentence from the Executive Summary: *"Ethical issues, individual privacy, and organizational integrity were rated as issues most important to the PR industry." [page 3]*

Within the study itself, "Respondents were asked to what extent they agree that the top management or CEO of their organization believes

---

[15] Excerpts from the PRSA: BACON'S 2006 STATE OF THE PR PROFESSION OPINION SURVEY. © 2007 Bacon's Information, Inc. The full study is available at www.bacons.com/

that Public Relations contributes to moving the organization forward in terms of three aspects: 1) reputation of the organization, 2) market share, and 3) financial success/sales." (page 4) Reputation was seen as the principle contribution PR makes in the eyes of management.

It is very encouraging that these public relations professionals feel that their priority is to maintain the reputation of their employers. Too often our discipline is seen as focused on publicity and spinning the company's misdeeds. I think this is another misconception generated by the minority of bad guys who show up in the media. I believe that most corporate entities and their communications professionals are closer to the ideal ethical business model than the barracuda model we see and hear so much about.

A less encouraging but still supportive view comes from a 2006 global survey of over 1,800 communication professionals by the International Association of Business Communicators Research Foundation (IABC). According to an IABC release[16] posted on their website, the new study, "The Business of Truth: A Guide to Ethical Communication," a majority of respondents agreed that ethical considerations are a vital part of executive decision-making and that PR and communication professionals should advise management on ethical matters. However, the research uncovered a clear divide between communicators on whether or not they should act as the principal ethical conscience or counsel in an organization.

On one side of the divide are those who believe that ethics and corporate reputation concerns go hand-in-hand, making ethical counsel a natural component of public relations and communications. On the other side are practitioners who believe that they are not positioned to be the primary advisors to management on ethics because of the complex nature of the issues (which are embedded in operating rules and regulations) and that such critical responsibilities should fall under the legal or compliance functions.

That is, of course, the last place ethical issues should be decided. Ethics is not about compliance, it's not about what you can get away with, it is about doing the right thing. I suspect that those expressing this view are from the "PR stands for press release" school of thinking.

---

[16] © 2007 International Association of Business Communicators.
One Hallidie Plaza, Suite 600 San Francisco, CA 94102 USA

Shannon A. Bowen, Ph.D., principal investigator of the research team and assistant professor at the University of Maryland, observed, "An encouraging finding of this study is that 65% of the sample reported having some influence in their dominant coalitions, with 30% of those practitioners telling us that they report directly to the CEO. Clearly PR holds influence at the policy level, a significant improvement over past research findings."

The research also revealed that while communicators often do play the role of ethics counsel or core values manager in their organizations, less than 30% of the respondents had received any education or training in ethics. Further, 63 % of communicators said that their current employers did not provide them with any additional ethics training or education such as seminars and workshops. ಈ

CHAPTER THIRTY

THE CONTRARIANS
Puncturing their balloons!

There are those who are openly opposed to any activity not focused on their vision of how to maximize profit. They generally fall into the Scrooge & Marley business model. Any suggestion that businesses have responsibilities beyond their bottom line is met with a hearty "Bah, humbug." I am indebted to *Firms of Endearment* author David Wolfe for outing one of these, the Free Enterprise Action Fund. The following comes directly from the fund's website:

> *The Free Enterprise Action Fund is the first mutual fund dedicated to providing both financial and pro-free enterprise ideological returns to investors.*
>
> *Why invest in the Free Enterprise Action Fund? Left-wing social and political activists are harnessing the power, resources and influence of publicly-owned corporations to advance their social and political agendas. (1) Frustrated by their failure to advance their agendas in the public political process, these activists use capitalism against capitalism under the guise of "corporate social responsibility" and "socially responsible investing." (2) Their movement threatens shareholder value and the American system of free enterprise.*
>
> *Leveraging its status as an institutional shareholder in hundreds of America's largest companies, the Fund aims to defend free enterprise from the Left's use of capitalism against capitalism.*
>
> *Our Core Principle. "The social responsibility of a business is to increase its profits." [Milton Friedman, Winner of the 1976 Nobel Prize in Economics] The Free Enterprise Action Fund is the first mutual fund dedicated to providing both financial and pro-free enterprise ideological returns to investors.*[17]

On the FoE website David points out that the Free Enterprise Action Fund doesn't practice what it preaches:

---

[17] Source: Free Enterprise Action Fund website, accessed 5/2/07
http://www.freeenterpriseactionfund.com/

Interestingly, FEAC doesn't eschew companies that proudly maintain a social agenda. Five of their investments are cited in our book as FoEs. How pure are these chaps, anyway? One of their larger investments is Johnson & Johnson (an FoE) whose widely applauded Credo – drafted long before corporate activists were anyone's worry – lists shareholders last in its enumerated list of beliefs and dedicated efforts.

These guys ought to fund the development of a time machine and take a one-way trip to the 19th century. They are wildly out of touch with business realities in the 21st century.

Take a look at the Johnson & Johnson Credo:

> *We believe our first responsibility is to the doctors, nurses and patients, to mothers and fathers and all others who use our products and services. In meeting their needs everything we do must be of high quality.*

> *We must constantly strive to reduce our costs in order to maintain reasonable prices.*

> *Customers' orders must be serviced promptly and accurately.*

> *Our suppliers and distributors must have an opportunity to make a fair profit.*

> *We are responsible to our employees, the men and women who work with us throughout the world. Everyone must be considered as an individual. We must respect their dignity and recognize their merit. They must have a sense of security in their jobs. Compensation must be fair and adequate, and working conditions clean, orderly and safe. We must be mindful of ways to help our employees fulfill their family responsibilities. Employees must feel free to make suggestions and complaints. There must be equal opportunity for employment, development and advancement for those qualified.*

> *We must provide competent management, and their actions must be just and ethical.*

*We are responsible to the communities in which we live
and work and to the world community as well. We must
be good citizens – support good works and charities and
bear our fair share of taxes. We must encourage civic
improvements and better health and education.*

*We must maintain in good order the property we are
privileged to use, protecting the environment and natural
resources.*

*Our final responsibility is to our stockholders. Business
must make a sound profit. We must experiment with new
ideas. Research must be carried on, innovative programs
developed and mistakes paid for. New equipment must be
purchased, new facilities provided and new products
launched. Reserves must be created to provide for
adverse times. When we operate according to these
principles, the stockholders should realize a fair return.*

*If these guys were authentic, they would dump J&J immediately,
for its Credo runs solidly against the Friedman dictum that the
only social responsibility of a company is to create profits for
its owners. The J&J Credo was drafted 60 years ago, about 25
years before Friedman made his celebrated remarks about the
only social responsibility of companies.[18]*

As I point out in the Introduction, Friedman's statement is fine as far
as it goes. The question is how do you maximize profit? The ethical
business model has always been the best way to maximize profit,
but documentation of that fact acceptable to Friedman and other
economists has become available only recently.

Milton Friedman was above all else a scholar. Would such a man ignore
new evidence and continue to hold to the beliefs he espoused in the
New York Times in the fall of 1970? I think not. I believe if he were
still alive, Friedman would have amended his thinking the moment he
examined the evidence available today. I am wary of those who attempt
to co-opt the thinking of an earlier era and use the status of the author
to validate their point, especially when it is so obvious that they are
hypocritical ideologues who do not practice what they preach.

---

[18] Firms of Endearment website, accessed 5/2/07 http://firmsofendearment.typepad.com/ © 2007

About the same time that *Firms of Endearment* by two academics and a writer was published, two academics and an investment company CEO released a study that seems to contradict the FoE findings. Deniz Anginer from the University of Michigan, Meir Statman from Santa Clara University, and Kenneth L. Fisher, Chairman, CEO & Founder of Fisher Investments, Inc. in Woodside, California, did such an analysis of the companies on *Fortune* magazine's "Most Admired" list.

In a twenty-nine-page report they compared the stocks of *Fortune's* most admired and most despised companies. They went back nearly a quarter century and found that the good guys and the bad guys did about the same. Actually, according to their study the bad guys did slightly better than the good guys over that period.

The top twenty on the latest "Most Admired" *Fortune* list includes seven (underlined) of those found among the twenty-eight profiled in *Firms of Endearment*: 1) General Electric, 2) Starbucks, 3) Toyota, 4) Berkshire Hathaway, 5) Southwest Airlines, 6) FedEx, 7) Apple, 8) Google, 9) Johnson & Johnson, 10) Procter & Gamble, 11) Goldman Sachs Group, 12) Microsoft, 13) Target, 14) 3M, 15) Nordstrom, 16) UPS, 17) American Express, 18) Costco, 19) PepsiCo., 19) Wal-Mart Stores (tie).[19]

While some of the companies on this list that did not make the FoE cut came close and are admirable companies, others are clearly not. How could the authors of *Firms of Endearment* find that the companies they chose "outperformed the broad market (S&P 500) by more than 8-1," when this study of the *Fortune* lists shows such a dramatically different outcome?

It seems obvious to me that two crucial factors missing in the *Fortune* ranking methodology make it unsuitable as an investment guide. They list the basics of their methodology on page 3 of their report:

> *The (Fortune) survey published in March 2006 included 611 companies in 70 industries. Fortune asked the 10,000 senior executives, directors and securities analysts who responded to the survey to rate the ten largest companies in their industries on eight attributes of reputation, using a scale of zero (poor) to ten (excellent).*

---

[19] Source: CNN.com, accessed 3/7/07

The attributes were quality of management; quality of products or services; innovativeness; long-term investment value; financial soundness; ability to attract, develop, and keep talented people; responsibility to the community and the environment; and wise use of corporate assets.

The most obvious reason the rankings in the *Fortune* studies are of little use in the comparison they are attempting to make is the universe. "Senior executives, directors and securities analysts" hardly constitute a cross section of stakeholders in the economy. Add to that the attributes used to rank these companies. Attributes that give little notice to those found in companies who strive to follow an ethical business model. On top of that, the *Fortune* study gave added weight to the opinions of those within the industry when voting on their peers. Now there's a way to elicit unbiased responses.

Mirror, mirror on the wall, who is the fairest of them all? Depends on what you are looking for. Ask a take-no-prisoners executive and that's the kind of company he will admire. Ask a stock market type who feeds on market churn and she will go for the companies she can keep trading.

The only thing the universe used in the *Fortune* study fits is their dream circulation base. And who can blame them for reaching out to their own?

☙

CHAPTER THIRTY-ONE

CAESAR'S WIFE
Julie Baby got it right 2,000 years ago.

There are few beings on the planet whose faith exceeds mine when it comes to the ability of mankind to solve the mysteries of the universe. I am the ultimate early adopter. If there is a new gadget, I have to have it. A new idea, I have to explore it. "Impossible" rarely crosses my lips except when it comes to the basic laws of physics.

The laws of nature are not going to change. Water is not going to run up hill; all of that physics stuff is set in stone. Human nature is not likely to change any time soon. We are not going to be able to pass laws that will create an ethical culture in business, or anywhere else. Individuals arrive at their workplace already equipped with either a set of rules for ethical behavior they have been taught, or with a dog-eat-dog attitude they have picked up, or with not a clue about the whole thing. If they lack an ingrained desire to do the right thing, nothing will compel them to do it unless it can be demonstrated that doing the right thing is in their own self-interest. A company may publish a "code of ethics," but it is not worth the paper it takes out of the copy machine if it is ignored. Keep in mind that Enron had what may have been the most elegant code of ethics ever.

Laws, rules, and policies cannot create ethical behavior.

Let's look at another area that, while necessarily governed by law, has proven impossible to fence in, taxes. No matter what, loopholes are found to circumvent the intent of the law. So more laws are passed and the authorities create ever more complex rules and interpretations. Do all the tax laws on the books from the smallest governmental entity to the United States Congress close all the loopholes?

Absolutely not!

Our tax code may be the most convoluted use of the English language ever contrived. But there are armies of tax types out there looking for ways around the laws. It's a game that never ends. Likewise, ethics is often not clear-cut; the right thing is not always obvious. That's why codes, if needed at all, need to be simple. Ethics is a culture, not a list of hard and fast rules or laws.

Remember what laws do. They draw a line in the sand that defines what society is willing to let you get away with. There are consequences for crossing any of those lines, but that leaves lots of room for unsavory behavior between what the law allows and what is ethical. We even set up a series of lines in the sand to determine how serious an infraction might be. The ethical position is way north of all this.

Ethics come into play at an entirely different level. What's more, even ethical lines are in shifting sand. Ultimately ethics is an attitude, a culture, a way of life, a climate, if you will. You can't legislate any of those attributes. You can't make a list or create a test.

That's why it's important that ethics emanate from the top. There are ethical individuals in every organization, but business models are molded at the top and they flow down, encouraging and empowering those in the trenches.

The ultimate example of this concept was set two thousand years ago. Do you remember the story about Caesar's wife? As the Maximus Dude in the Roman Empire, Julius Caesar was also High Priest of the official state religion. He was married to a legendary beauty, Pompeia, who as First Lady headed the highly secretive ladies' night out known as the rites of "Bona Dea." Roughly translated, it's "Good Goddess."

No one knows what went on at these closed-door shindigs, just that they had a very strict chicks-only rule. So when a notorious womanizer, Publius Clodius Pulcher (PCP), was discovered at the event disguised as a woman enjoying whatever he was enjoying, Pompeia, as the Goddess du jour, took the rap. She failed the Bona Dea test big-time. There were rumors that maybe she had not been a totally "Good" Goddess.

Even though PCP was put to trial and the court found him to be hanky-panky free, Caesar divorced Pompeia, reportedly declaring, "Caesar's wife must be above suspicion." Thereby establishing a benchmark for ethical behavior that two thousand years later still sounds pretty good. The leader must set the standard, if their team is to have a standard to emulate. Leaders must be above suspicion.

Conversely, no set of laws nor any high-minded ethics code will assure ethical behavior. Let's take the legal backlash unleashed by Ebbers, Lay, Rigas, et al. In 2002 the Congress gave us Sarbanes-Oxley (SOX).

This law is intended to rein in corporate schemers and give the public and investors a fighting chance to understand what's going on in the corporate entities that dominate our economy and govern our working lives.

While it may have made it harder for the bad guys –who I truly believe to be in the minority– SOX has mainly served to distract corporate leaders and enrich their accounting and legal counsel. In so doing it absorbs billions from our economy that ultimately comes right out of our pockets. It is one more failed attempt to legislate something that I hope this book will help to convince even the bad guys out there could be better achieved by instituting an ethical business model. If every business was focused on the advantages of an ethical business model, they could make more money without hanky-panky and SOX would be unnecessary along with most of the tax code.

In the end there is no such thing as an ethical entity, be it a business or any other organization. There are only ethical people, led by an ethical individual, all working together to search out and apply the right thing day in and day out. That's why I call it an "Ethical Business Model." A model that is a lot more fun to be a part of, and one that is demonstrably more profitable.

Play Nice, Make Money. ๛

THE BOTTOM LINE

BY THESE SIGNS SHALL YE KNOW THEM

The narratives in the preceding chapters have illustrated the triumphs and tragedies of a few organizations and individuals. To provide (as Captain Barbossa would say) some "guidelines," here are signs to look for in assessing whether an Ethical Business Model underpins a leader's style and therefore the culture of a company or organization. And keep in mind, it's all about leadership.

Eleven Traits of an Ethical Leader

✓ They focus on the right thing and act to make it so.

✓ They provide transparency.

✓ They solicit the wisdom of all those with an interest in the organization and weigh it into their decisions.

✓ They engender a culture of trust.

✓ They defer authority to those closest to the task.

✓ They credit those who make positive contributions.

✓ They take ownership of mistakes and errors as opportunities to learn and improve.

✓ They have the courage to make unpopular decisions.

✓ They treat everyone with respect and courtesy.

✓ They recognize that what's best for all stakeholders is best for the organization.

✓ They lead by example.

৪৩

ACKNOWLEDGEMENTS

I never thought I would write a book. I've been writing for decades, but I have always seen myself and still see myself as an essayist. About five hundred words defines my comfort zone. And there is no place more comfortable than a place where those five hundred words might make a difference. Like many such opportunities my involvement in business ethics took a long-cherished viewpoint and opened a door to help move it to another level. So I've cobbled together some OPEDs published elsewhere with some new work and reviews of books that touch on the subject.

I am grateful to all those who have given me permission to reprint portions of their work. Especially to the publishers of the public relations journal *Bulldog Reporter* and its editor, Brian Pittman, who have been kind enough to allow me to include materials first published there. Without Brian there would have been no opportunity to broaden my interest in this subject and certainly no book. His review of an early draft was also a major factor in sharpening my viewpoint and presentation.

I am also beholden to many others who reviewed drafts and helped to refine the work. Some cheered me on; others offered suggestions that added to both my thinking and the content. I'm especially appreciative of the support of my daughter Carol Newman McKibben, an accomplished writer in her own right whose work far outshines my efforts.

I owe all the members of my family. My parents and all those who preceded them. Our wonderful children who have the ethics gene and have been more successful in applying it than I ever hoped to be. And the ultimate reward, the grandchildren who add a dimension to my life filled with fascination, wonder, and discovery.

Then there are all the people I've worked with over the years. The clients and associates in a multitude of enterprises. Those who have shown the way and a few towering figures who have filled me with awe and inspired me. Most of all I owe thanks to those who had faith in me beyond my own faith. Their trust and the tasks they empowered me to undertake helped to make my life worthwhile.

I cannot overstate Alfred Kirchhofer's contribution to my life. This giant was in his eighth decade when I arrived in Buffalo. His wisdom and the standards he set reinforced the best in me. He was a communications pioneer, although he always saw himself as a newspaper man. His contributions to that craft included the rewrite concept utilizing the new-fangled telephone to get the story back to the newsroom instead of losing time hoofing it back. He latched onto every new idea and promotional concept. He took an also-ran newspaper out of a pack of a dozen or more and made it the unchallenged leader in the community.

He was a founder of the National Press Club in Washington and a power in business and politics for decades. And yet, unlike others, Kirchhofer never saw the power as his. He saw himself as a representative of those who read the paper he built and edited. His impact on Radio and TV was significant as well, and it was there our lives intersected. I was lucky to count him as mentor and friend for nearly twenty years. An associate once said, "A.H.K. can be summed up in one word, integrity." True.

Many who preceded me in this effort to bring the ethical business model to the fore are referenced and quoted extensively in this book. I am especially indebted to David Wolfe and his associates, whose seminal work on the Firms of Endearment project put legs under my long-held faith in this model. I feel like one of the singers in the back row of a choir, adding my voice to the chorus, enchanted by the soloists and hopeful that my modest effort will add a little something meaningful.

No discussion of the ethical business model can omit the work of Peter Drucker. A vital component of this model is the concept of bottom-up management that he pioneered. His work in the '30s and '40s brought the idea into the mainstream business community.

His concepts encourage a culture that engages and empowers everyone in an organization, turning them into a team, bridging the "us vs. them" mentality that undermines trust and slows productivity. Peter Drucker created the very foundation of the modern day ethical business model. And too, you have to admire a man who greeted his wife every time they met during their seventy years together as, "My Darling."

The talented Catherine Kaiser of the Kaiser Design Studio transformed my clumsy ideas into a handsome design. The cover font is EAGLEFEATHER, created by the P22 Type Foundry based on the work of Frank Lloyd Wright as a part of their ongoing mission to revive historical fonts. My thanks to P22 Senior Partner Richard Kegler for allowing its use.

Finally, my thanks to my associate, John Manzella. Without our long-term association, there is no way this book would exist.

W. T. McKibben
Buffalo, New York
7.7.7

Printed in the United States
203384BV00003B/232-315/A

9 781604 024128